THE DARK EMPTY CAVE

SHORT FICTION, POETRY, AND SERMONS

WILLIAM C. BETCHER

Edited by
HELEN HARDT

THE DARK EMPTY CAVE

SHORT FICTION, POETRY, AND SERMONS

William C. Betcher

Edited By
Helen Hardt

HS
HARDT & SONS ♥

HS

HARDT & SONS ♥

🏵 Created with Vellum

For Daddy

"He gave to me a gift I know I never can repay."
~ Dan Fogelberg, "The Leader of the Band"

and

In memory of

William John Betcher

and

Helen Marie Hardt Betcher

One man's search for God...

He stood near the exit of the dark empty cave, but he never walked through.

Though this volume contains sermons, it's not a book about religion. It's about a journey one man never completed because he got in his own way. The message is timeless and particularly applicable today.

EDITOR'S NOTE

These pieces were written mostly in the sixties, so it goes without saying that some of the terms used and ideas presented aren't politically correct. I've chosen to leave them as they are as a testament to the era in which they were written.

The cited works of Robert Frost and Walt Whitman are in the public domain.

INTRODUCTION

Today would have been my father's eighty-fourth birthday.

William Charles Betcher was a brilliant man.

He was an equally troubled man.

I don't know much about his childhood, but the little I do know is far from idyllic. I recall one story my mother told me when I was a young teen. My paternal grandmother was a fanatic about keeping a spotless home—such a fanatic that she tied her young son to a tree in the yard so she could clean in peace, secure in the knowledge that he wouldn't run off and also wouldn't come inside and trample his dirty country boy feet onto her clean floor.

Later, I learned more about his less than ideal childhood, but there is still much I don't know that died with him.

Billy was a beautiful child. "You was the pretty one," my grandmother from the hills of Pennsylvania used to say, when comparing him to his younger sister. He was a smart and curious little boy. Born with a lazy eye, he wore an eye patch for over a year. "He was the sweetest little boy," my grandmother told my mother, "until he had to wear that eye patch."

Billy excelled at school and loved to read and write. He was also a gifted artist and drew portraits in pencil and ink. To his average parents, none of this made sense. They simply couldn't relate. They made fun of his intelligence, laughing at him and calling him birdbrain.

As he reached adolescence, his struggle with his sexual orientation began. Though he dated women and eventually married my mother, leading to my sister and me, he was always a gay man at heart and eventually came out in the seventies.

Before then, however, he immersed himself in baseball, journalism, and theater in high school, while tapping out stories on his typewriter. During college, he continued to write. Of his short story *The Dark Empty Cave*, one English professor wrote:

Peculiar! And excellent. If you can expand this to 200 (or 300) pages, and not flaw it by losing the spirit of Bar Hollow and its people, do so. You write (at your best) like a true poet. You have good characters—real, living, human. The rawness of life is acutely personal.

Though he'd written the story during his high school years and then repurposed it for a college assignment, the paper indicates it was turned in late. Classic Bill. My father was lazy to a fault. He couldn't get it together, but the truth is, I don't think he ever really tried. Throughout his life, he blamed his childhood, others, and circumstances for his failures. He tried therapy several times, but it was never successful.

At college graduation, a friend told Bill of his plans to attend graduate school to study English. Bill said to him, "I wish I could do that, but I've already signed my life away."

He could have, but instead he went to Trinity Lutheran Seminary in Columbus, Ohio. Bill would be a minister.

I used to wonder why my father chose this path when his true love was writing. He always talked about "my book." The book never got written. He could never pull himself together enough to get it done. The pieces in this volume were written mostly in the sixties. While my father continued to preach well into the seventies, until he and my mother divorced and he resigned from the ministry, very little of that work was original. His laziness took over, and he relied on published outlines rather than his own gifts.

And he *was* gifted. His writing has a lushness that I can never hope to duplicate. He was my first mentor, encouraging me in my writing from the time I learned how to form letters with a fat pencil in the first grade. Soon I was writing stories, and he gave me a metal file box with "Helen's Story Box" written on it in permanent marker.

Despite this, however, my relationship with my father was never a good one. I looked exactly like him; was named after his mother, with whom he had a love-hate relationship; and as the first born, I took my mother's attention away from him. This perfect storm led him to project his own self-hatred onto me. I suffered years of emotional abuse from him.

Though our relationship was toxic in many ways, I give credit where credit is due. My father encouraged me to write, and though I took some detours along the way, I eventually did what he never could.

I published a book.

Then another.

To date, I've published nearly forty novel-length works and various shorter ones, all with about a tenth of my father's talent. Talent, after all, is nothing without the hard work to back it up— a lesson my father never learned due to his inability to leave the past in the past.

My father wrote to me sporadically throughout my college years and adulthood. His letters were usually a bizarre combination of effusive compliments and guilt trips. When I decided to attend law school, he said it was a mistake, that I should be writing. I responded that I needed to make a living and that he couldn't live his dream through me. Looking back, I see he was giving me the advice he didn't take himself after his own college graduation. Law school, of course, wasn't a mistake. Though I practiced for only two years, I met my husband there, and we're still together thirty-one years and two sons later. A path isn't always laid out in a straight line.

Interest in writing sparked again in my father after the birth of my older son, his first grandchild. He wanted to write a memoir in a series of *Letters to Eric.* However, like his book that never got written, this project fizzled out well before completion.

I've spent a lot of my adult life considering who my father truly was. He was so lost for much of his life, and he never had a satisfying relationship before or after coming out. For a while, I believed he chose the path of the ministry to "heal himself" of his homosexuality. Being a gay man in the sixties was a lot more difficult than it is today. While I still think that may be partially true, I've come to a new conclusion.

After my father passed away, I read his stories again. Then I read his sermons. He went a little fire and brimstone sometimes, and he rarely practiced in life what he preached from the pulpit. I don't agree with everything he wrote, but one theme is abundantly clear throughout every word of his stories and sermons.

He was searching for God.

Perhaps if he'd found what he searched for so profoundly, he'd have been able to free himself from the self-hatred that plagued him. Perhaps he wouldn't have squandered his talent and lived a life of mostly unhappiness. Instead, he trapped himself in endless victimhood and refused to find his way out.

He never learned the ultimate truth—to find God, you must first look inside yourself, even if you don't like what you see. *Especially* if you don't like what you see.

I saw him a few days before he passed away.

So much transpired between us during the half a century we were in each other's lives, and to be honest, most of it wasn't good. I needed to face him, though. He seemed to be holding onto a life he no longer wanted. If I could give him peace, I felt an obligation to do so—for myself as much as for him.

My once handsome and robust father had become a shadow, but he smiled when he saw me. He told me I was beautiful, and I held his hand.

"I forgive you, Daddy," I said to him, "and now you need to forgive yourself. Forgive yourself and go if you want to. It's okay. Everything is okay."

Forty-eight hours later, he was gone. He died knowing I loved him, and I also believe he loved me as well as he could.

The contents of this book were written over fifty years ago, but as I read through them, I realized how important their message still is today.

We're not that different.

The world has the same problems, the same issues.

Perhaps God—or the light or the truth or whatever you choose to think of as divine—can be part of the solution.

My father had to leave this life to find his way out of the dark empty cave—the metaphor for the emptiness in his soul.

The light was always there. My father stood near the exit of the cave but chose not to walk through. He never learned that the past doesn't have to rule your life. The world's struggles don't have to rule your life. Victimhood and self-hatred don't have to rule your life.

There's always a way out.

Helen Hardt
December 3, 2020

SHORT FICTION

THE DARK EMPTY CAVE

1

T he rapid beating of a young heart seems slow when a wide awake boy waits for the hilltop trees to silhouette the first daylight shadows. Morning appears first at the top of a Pennsylvania hill, gently rolls over the wet treetops, and snakes its way down along the mulched leaves and briars until it illuminates the white mist hugging the green-carpeted valleys.

Impatiently, I sat on a rotted maple stump with my bare feet buried in the cool sand of Pine Creek. I was alone—lost in the business of thinking boyish thoughts—listening for the first rooster, barking dog, cawing blackbird, or splashing carp to herald the dawn.

In the distance towered the phantom shadow of the boney pile belonging to the Bar Hallow Mine. I marveled at the gaseous flames flinging their hideous patterns across the top and sides of the clinkered mountain, causing miniature rainbows to appear through the morning fog. Scratched and bleeding, I often arrived home a burnished black after climbing in search of one of those flaming gullies that made a ghoulish mystery out of each summer night. Loud lectures and leather poundings were the only rewards of my flights in search of phantasy. Morning mist still enveloped the little green smoke-house a few hundred yards away, but the clean cherry smoke drifting from its newly stoked fires invaded the valley like morning incense.

A wild yelp and frantic scurrying among the dry weeds told me that my old dog had either located or stumbled onto a rabbit. Old Henry was not much of a hunter, but he enjoyed out-foxing himself and running down the endless trails leading to nowhere. What more could a guy ask for in a dog?

The ancient black Model A truck was parked at the top of the driveway leading to the house that was my summer home. The creaky old truck was always perched there so that Pop Charlie—that's my Grandfather—could coast her into starting on the cool mornings. If the Model A wouldn't chug into life by the time it coasted into the stable yard, Pop would become a variegated red—*damn the universe, Henry Ford, and the Democrats in Congress.*

The Dodge, spanking new with its original paint and tires, sat solitary in the garage. It only saw daylight once or twice each week when it was carefully backed out of the garage and dusted off with a fluffy Turkish towel. The chrome was even gobbed with Vaseline to keep it from pitting or something. My uncle's yellow convertible was parked under the acorn shading the walled pump porch. He was too bull-headed to park elsewhere, even if all the birds in Allegheny County did roost in that acorn tree.

"What the hell?" I said aloud, slamming a rock into the creek in front of me. Three lousy cars and not one of the slobs will roll out of the sack long enough to go to church!

The water vibrations, circling outward, had a calming effect on my rash early morning thoughts. Imagine me thinking about a church! Well, that wasn't so strange. I did know the twenty-third psalm and the Our Father by heart, and it was Sunday. I reached to the ground, picked up a round flat stone, and held it in the palm of my hand. I wondered if that stone knew it was Sunday, not even thinking that it had known years of Sundays, hot, cold, and buried. My wrist snapped out quickly. The stone flew from my hand and skipped once, twice, three times over the water and sank to the bottom downstream with a *kerplop*. *Not bad*, I thought.

I took my feet out of their earthy blanket, rubbed them free of mud and sand on the cold marsh grass growing along the creek bank. After whistling for Old Henry, I walked toward the dam that used to hold the water of my swimming hole. A few years before, Pop Charlie had smashed it after the accident.

Alybert Reymer, a kind of anemic kid cousin of mine, was swimming with our gang on one of those stinking hot summer evenings. To make a dull story short, he stepped on a broken jar that he couldn't see in the muddy water and cut the devil out of his foot. He screamed as we dragged him to the bank. Early evening moonlight illuminated a trail of black blood leading from the creek to his foot, where it was throbbing out like a geyser. Alybert wasn't saying anything then—just wriggling back and forth on the stones as if a rattler had him by the hind end. Then he screamed up and down the scale worse than Lily Pons.

"Sonny! Run and get Pop Charlie!" The words escaped my throat in a hoarse whisper.

My blond-haired companion stood there looking straight ahead. His eyes were glazed with fear. Sonny's bronze body looked as white as Adam standing naked in the moonlight.

"For Christ's sake, put your clothes on and get help!" My hands were cold and shaking. Sweat and hot tears poured from my face.

Sonny finally moved off and became a shadow.

Alybert remained motionless, the blood pumping out of the

deep gash in his foot. His eyes were open—staring through the brave façade I was attempting to maintain. *Help me*, they said. *Help me, I love you, help me!* Alybert was quivering in a hellish throbbing rhythm as the life juice gushed from his body.

There was nothing I could do. I didn't have a belt, a rope, a vine, or even a lousy piece of string for a tourniquet. I swallowed hard, fighting the lump of spittle in my throat.

"Take it easy, Alley. Sonny's gettin' Pop."

My choking words were intruders on the night silence. *Take it easy*. What a foolish thing to say. Contradictions overcrowded my beating brain. I saw the entire world topple end over end among the clouds of searing reds, blues, and blacks that colored my thoughts.

A fish, probably disturbed by a hunger-lusting crayfish, splashed to the distant surface.

Why did Alley have to come tonight? I had worried about Alybert ever since I learned in school that he spelled his name with a Y. Alley was different than the rest of the guys, never having any interest in our cruddy jokes, in smoking weeds behind the post office, or dancing with the girls in the gym at lunch time. He was an all right guy though, always smiling, lending money, and reading poetry.

Alybert groaned, attempted to move, and stretched out stiffly. His cold and shaking body fought each pumping jerk of his heart. A gurgle came from his throat. The eyes were no longer open, but closed, almost bursting in pain. Alley was in a state of shock. What did I know about shock?

There was nothing I could do.

"Hang on, Alley! Please hang on!" I lifted his hand and held it tightly, reaching for some sign of life in Alley other than the warm coagulum at his feet.

His fingers were long and bony, just right for playing the piano. Alley liked the piano. Moonlight reflected brilliantly from his gold class ring. It was the one he had bought after washing windows down at the store for three months. Alley thought a lot of that ring.

My friend was hurt and in pain, and there was nothing I could do. I thought of prayer, but that didn't work. There was not anything much that I could say and no god to say a prayer to. Grandma used to pray with her Bible and quilting hoops on her lap. I knew that there was such a thing as prayer, but no one ever had the time to teach me while I was young, and they all knew they couldn't teach me anything now.

The moon escaped behind an unseen cloud, changing the world into a dark empty cave. I held tightly to Alley's hand and swabbed with forehead with a wet handkerchief.

There was nothing I could do!

That is what I told Alley's mother and father and sister and god.

That is what I told Alley as I visited his coffin at the Lutheran Church two days later.

2

_____

Having passed the death hold, I cut my way through the thorny bushes that had blundered in wild disorder across the rutted path. It was almost daylight now. A field mouse darted across the path, behind a stone, and into a mud-caked hole with three quick movements. Birds fluttered over my head, leaping from twig to limb on the black-barked cherry trees. The sewage smell of stagnant creek water everywhere mixed with sweeter smells of mature hay and alfalfa. With a twisting splash, a moccasin slid gracefully into the water and pushed soundlessly downstream, its blunt head effortlessly searching every rock.

I walked to the cast iron steps that led up to the bridge crossing Pine Creek. Three of its corrugated steps had rusted away, and the long four-inch pipes that supported the bridge were lashed together with a long steel cable corroded green by mine gases.

I called Old Henry.

After giving one sharp yipe in answer to my command, the childish old dog bounded toward the bridge. Henry's golden spaniel ears flopped as he leaped high to see over the tall weeds.

Finally, the panting white dog reached me and parked his haunches at my feet.

It was crazy, but this apathetic mass of mats and dripping saliva was one of my best friends. I reached down and pulled his ears and scratched under his chin. I had always been of the opinion that this ancient animal was more human than most people, and that far too many humans were proud of having the characteristics of dogs. Old Henry grunted as I carried him across the rotted planking of the swaying bridge. He licked my face. His pus-filled eyes told me the job was well done. Henry padded into the brush in a chaotic frenzy, chasing another imaginary creature that he was much too old to catch. The wart on his eye was getting larger every day. Henry would be blind by next summer. *Damn shame,* I thought.

I sneezed convulsively. Birds flew in many directions, chiding me for this invasion of their privacy. Ironically, I had always been allergic to dog hair.

Lost within myself, I missed the ethereal beauty of the orange sun's first appearance above the blue mist of the Bar Hallow bony pile. Ignoring the natural surroundings that were my environment during these solitary wanderings, I did not bother to look. What a pathetic realization. Already I felt I had seen all the natural beauty that a country existence could offer.

Even though I was lost in thought, my feet took me along the winding path to my oldest refuge—the oil well. The chug of its mighty engine and the shrill creaking of its pumping arm became steadily louder and woke me to consciousness as I approached the clearing where the well house lay. The morning smelled of decaying wood and wet mulch. I always tingled with excitement at the first sight of the well—the odd-shaped oily shack with its slanting tin roof, the orange encrusted derrick and its ladder reaching skyward, the deafening *boom-boom* of the coughing iron horse making the well house vibrate with each rhythmic pumping throb.

Yet there was an undefinable humbleness of nature surrounding this throbbing giant and the woods it commanded. This was one of the first places Pop Charlie had taken me as a young boy. Pop was an oil-man—a pumper for the South Penn Oil Company. The steaming mass of iron and steel rearing in front of me was his ol' girlfriend, Rosie O'Grady. Most of Pop Charlie's love for Rosie had sloughed off onto me. This was the one spot I chose whenever I had any serious thinking to do, for here I felt closer to myself and the absolute.

When Pop used to stop the engine, the woody silence was unnatural and far worse than the turbulent and living Rosie O'Grady. Without the steady beating of the machinery, even the lightest breeze seemed to voice a barren song as it whistled through the cracked boards of the musty well shack.

Pumping the well required all of the skill Pop Charlie had learned during his lifetime, but in those days it was exciting for me to watch. Armed with an oil can and a greasy rag, I used to crawl beneath the warm engine to fill oil cups and wipe off any excess slime that might fall on the belts. Meanwhile, Pop Charlie would have read the gauges, tightened the long red-rubber belts, and refueled the pilot burners.

As Pop started the engine, I stood aside and watched. To start the engine, he had to mount one of the massive wheels and —with his bulky strength, aided by the weight of his two-hundred-pound frame—open the vicious jaws of the machinery. Often, the hot engine would backfire in a sputtering cough, forcing him to jump from the spinning wheel. Pop's face would be beet-red and streaked black by the running rivers of sweat that appeared from under his railroad cap. After six or seven turns of the giant wheel, the engine began to choke, snort, and fire—its exhaust churning dusty clouds throughout the well house. Then, the belts began to move and the screeching pumping arm continued its business of sucking virgin oil from earth's hidden rivers. Pop Charlie would smile and gently pat the throbbing monster that was his sweetheart and friend. Once, Rosie O'Grady had backfired, throwing Pop broken and unconscious against the splintered ties that shackled the engine to the earth.

"A big machine is a man's best friend," he would say, "but don't you ever turn your back on one or you deserve to get kicked in the seat of the pants."

We would then box a few rounds and laugh like a couple of kids. Those were the days!

It was warmer now, close to eight o'clock I judged, squinting toward the sun. In one quick movement, I squashed a yellow bee biting angrily on my arm. A small red dot appeared in the center of the white bump rising from the bee sting. A mixture of spittle and mud quickly took away the itch.

Stretching myself out of the cool crabgrass that surrounded the well house with sporadic tufts of reddish green, I began to turn the pages of the testament I carried around in my shirt pocket. My gaze jumped rapidly across the double-columned squashed words of god, searching for meaning, understanding, and hope. I had begun to read from the Bible after Alley's death. I even read a little poetry when I was well-secluded from the gang and didn't have much else to do. Funny stuff, that fumbling mass of moods they call poetry! The Bible was different though, making a little bit of sense, even though the small print made me squint. Jesus, I would have died if Sonny or anyone else had caught me reading that stuff. Coming to the well to read had become a habit many years ago.

Before the accident, about the only thing that I ever had to do with religion was to tear down the *Jesus Saves* signs that queers had nailed to righteous telephone poles. One night,

Sonny and I took a can of red paint and re-lettered one of the signs to read *Jesus Saves Green Stamps*. The idea was not original, but few young artists' ideas are. Our sign disappeared mysteriously a couple of days later. The splintered pole looked naked without it.

When I was only a fourteen-year-old stud with a lousy case of pimples, I attended the Christian Missionary Church overlooking the turnpike. The Christian Missionaries never boasted of having the largest church in the county, but they indisputably possessed the loudest preacher in Western Pennsylvania.

Reverend Homer Potter was as big a man physically as folks said he was spiritually. Behind screened windows, closed doors, and in front of the store, Homer Potter was referred to affectionately as Fatso, the Old Windbag, Baggy Pants Potter, Hell's Angel, and Preach Potter. To his face, the blushing older ladies straightened their seems and called him Reverend Potter. Father Victor from Saint Killian's called him Mr. Potter, but for the most part, everyone who knew the man called him Preach.

"What are you doin' tonight?" Sonny asked that afternoon as we lay under the leaking oil pan of Pop Charlie's Model A.

"Oh, I thought that I'd go to church for a while," I said.

"Church!" Sonny grease-spotted grin leered at me through the dripping oil. "Holy crud, since when do *you* go to church? His blond crew-cut brushed the Ford's axle as he turned to enjoy my reaction.

"That my business, I think." My voice growled, quivered, and finally broke into the gravel tone of adolescence. *Hell*, I thought, *I guess a man has the right to go to church if he wants.*

Silence greeted the crimson that appeared at the base of my spine and rushed to the top of my head.

"Well, keep your plow clean," Sonny replied.

The tension prevailing between us was disturbed only by the

slap of the dripping crankcase. Religion is one subject never discussed by teenagers. Sonny and I were no different.

I attended Preach's prayer meeting that night because I wanted to walk Bumps Malley down Bar Hallow Road after the service to talk or something. Bumps Malley began to participate in my dreams long before I knew she was praying for my soul. One of her lungs was defective, causing her to cough when excited, but anyone with eyes could see that there was nothing much wrong with her. Bumps Malley lived up to her name to the very last inch.

A piano was playing softly within the red-brick church. I stood at the door, trying to work up enough manly courage to enter. Truck tires spun hot whining sounds on the pavement below. Four lanes of headlights cast grotesque shadows across the fenced pastures and Bar Hallow cornfields dotting the speedway. A light evening breeze fanned the bubbles of sweat on my forehead into ice-water rivulets.

After inhaling deeply three times, I straightened my tie and stepped into the sanctuary, edging toward the nearest pew as inconspicuously as possible. There were only about thirty people in the small room that night. Searching for Bumps Malley, I looked at every one of them. The wrinkled man beside me was bent in prayer, exhibiting his red leathery farmer's neck. A golden-curled baby yawned and kicked himself to sleep on his proud mother's lap. Already, she was big with another child. Her young husband had the pale white arms and black fingernails of a Bar Hallow miner. One lady was chewing gum in rhythm to the piano. A devil in short pants pinched his little sister and received a slap. Paint hanging in dirty yellow strips mixed with the black ceiling cobwebs. A chair, a piano, a pulpit, and thirty sleepy people were the only indications that I was in a church.

The service proceeded with rhythmic frenzy. The singing was distracting, especially when Margaret Benson contraltoed her way into the second verse of every hymn four bars ahead of her nearest rival, dragging the pianist and congregation after her. Elmer Porty stood and led the prayer.

I couldn't stand the endless monotone of monotonous thees and thous, so I let my mind wander. My hands were too sweaty to fold. They always used to sweat when I thought of Bumps Malley.

Preach stood and talked quietly for half an hour. None of his words impressed me as much as the fact that he used a black hairpin for a tie clip. Sinners were invited to the first pew as everybody hummed "I Need Thee Every Hour." Nobody moved.

I waited for Bumps at the door. All I had seen of her in church was the blond bush of her ponytail. A soft determined voice behind me made me jump.

"Do you want to be saved?" Homer Potter's god-glazed eyes were burning holes into my forehead as I turned to face the sound interrupting my thoughts.

"Not right now. Thanks," I managed to sputter.

"Oh, God, forgive this unfortunate sinner for refusing thine invitation to..."

It took me a moment to notice that he was praying, and much longer to realize that he was praying for me. On and one he prayed, giving neither god nor me a single bit of rest. I tightly closed my eyes and tried to conjure an excuse for leaving. Red and green circles electrified the back of my brain as Preach's words crashed into my consciousness like rolling drums.

"Ah...men!"

Silence is much harder to take than prayer. A hand was pulling me down the stone church steps into the pitch night and highway sounds. Bumps Malley was coughing and crying. We loved each other and I had refused her god.

Sweat rolled into my eyes. After I rubbed them, the trees blurred back into focus. Old Henry was standing at my feet and barking. They were coming again, just like they came every Sunday morning. To Old Henry, noise was as equally disturbing made by a friend as by an enemy. His stubby tail began to wag when Pop Charlie and Hans walked toward the noisy oil well. Their arms locked together, they were singing loudly—

Sweet Rosie O'Grady

Dropped her bra in the gravy...

Laughter rolled from within the well-house. Pop and Hans came every Sunday to drink, tell stories, and sleep it off under the protection of Rosie O'Grady. Eating and drinking provided the only entertainment they had ever known. The spell of my early morning thoughts was broken. I left my favorite meditation spot. Anyway, it was time for church, and I had to walk.

A white-shingled Lutheran church stood at the top of Bar Hallow hill. Its pointed green steeple could be seen for miles on any clear day. A freshly-painted barn could not have looked less like a church, but this little haven of love changed my life. Growing to love Divinity Lutheran Church was the finest thing that had ever happened to me.

After my experience with the Christian Missionaries, I resolved never to enter a church again, but Divinity Lutheran had been Alley's church. His mother asked me to attend a morning worship with her and I could not very well refuse. Prepared for the worst, I walked up the rutted driveway surrounding the obsolete old church. An hour later, I came out almost a Christian.

"I want you to have this," Alley's mother told me on my Confirmation Day. Her eyes were red raw.

I knew that she was crying inside. Trembling, she handed me Alybert's gold class ring.

"You can't give me this—" I started to say.

"Please, take it, and God be with you," she interrupted, turning and hurrying away.

Dozens of well-meaning folks shook my hand that morning. Looking cherub-like in a spring bonnet with yellow straw flowers, Bumps Malley stood happily at my side and helped me greet my new friends. The little white church and Christ stood inconspicuously in the background as I captured the limelight that Palm Sunday. Bumps Malley approved of me and my church, and I approved of the world. But—

Slop Willard hated my guts.

In Bar Hallow society, the name Willard was another symbol for gold. John Willard, Sr. had his money tied up in land, coal, oil, beer, and chicken feed. Two-thirds of Bar Hallow was either owned outright or held in mortgage by the house of Willard. Yet John Willard was loved by almost everyone, for he was an honest man. The only fault that he had was the two-hundred-pound piece of oily blubber that was his son.

Slop had everything that I didn't have—a big house on the hill, a motorcycle, a fast car, and loads of spending money.

But I had Bumps Malley.

"So our little brother has found religion," Slop wheezed through the fish-like opening above the first of numerous chins. He hitched his thumbs in the wide black belt that divided his stomach into separate pillows of lard-barrel fat. "Say a little prayer for us."

"Nah! I think he should sing a hymn," chided the money-sucking leeches who were Slop's friends.

"Shut up, you slimy bastard," I said. Involuntarily, I slapped him hard across the face, missing his mouth and poking my finger into his eye.

Slop Willard must have been as shocked as I was, for I got away with the whole business. Such were my feeble attempts at standing up for a religion I could not understand.

Nevertheless, I had sentenced myself to the task of evading Slop Willard and his friends. Nothing happened during the next two weeks, so I forgot about the whole mess and eventually laughed it off. There were more important things on my mind.

There was no moon the night Pop Charlie came over to the well to talk. Old Henry was asleep beside the soup bone Grandma had given him at dinner. I was lying on the damp grass, listening to the frog songs and watching fireflies wink their way across the thorny horizon.

Pop Charlie stood over me. The heavy breathing of calloused lungs told me of his presence.

"I don't like it," I said, turning to face him. "Rosie O'Grady doesn't seem the same without the noise."

"Ya can't bleed an oil well son," Pop replied. "They have to rest just like human beings. I'll start her up again on the first of the week."

I had known he would. Pop Charlie and I were only mouthing words to end the penetrating silence.

Heat lightning sparked the static sky. A distant airplane droned louder and louder behind the clouds and disappeared as slowly as it had come.

"I saw her tonight." Pop paused and blew his nose on the tail of his shirt. "She wants to talk to you."

"I don't ever want to see her again Tell her I'm happy here," I said vehemently.

Tears funneled into my eyes. What a damn, damn lie. I wanted to see her more than anybody in the whole world, even Bumps Malley.

"Christ, boy, she just sat there and cried tonight. Sat there, rocking and crying. I think she's aged three years in the past two months."

"How can I help it? She threw *me* out, didn't she?" My left eye twitched nervously.

"Good god, boy, she's all alone!" Pop Charlie's whiskey-toned words would have melted steel. "Have you forgotten that she is your mother?"

The world of my own creation collapsed. Pop Charlie walked away. Old Henry followed him.

I stumbled into the clearing in a blind rage. My face was scratched, torn, and bleeding from weaving through the brambled woods. Hot tears kept me from seeing, yet I was not crying. I was too old to cry.

A solitary figure was standing on a hangman's platform. A knotted rope was reaching from his neck. A naked white hangman appeared and laughed.

I was watching my own execution and I could not confess. A fiery fever scorched my brain, rupturing the thought vessels into thousands of tiny black furies of ice-cold fear.

I stopped at the swimming hole and bathed my hot face in the sewer water of Pine Creek.

"Alley! Alley!" My pleas became lost in the tangled underbrush of my own mind.

The drums crashed again. The hangman's laughter rolled out across the still water. He was standing in a pool of deep red running blood. Bony piano fingers reached for my hand and the ring.

Help me, help me, I need you, help me, chanted a guttural chorus of croaking frogs.

A dull throbbing blackness surrounded and enveloped me.

EPILOGUE

A Spirit woke the Materialist on a summer's night.
The first words spoken were harsh, yet pensive.
"How dare you sell my Church?
That little white building that has beheld so much of life, hope, and death,
That has aroused the glow of love in many lonely hearts,
That offered quiescence to many weary and hopeless Spirits.
Its old frame embodied the mourning women of three wars,
And now strains under the dragging feet of the men of the next war.
Some already bump their heads descending the creaky cellar stairs.
The motley lawn has long been a refuge for the misplaced of God's Creatures.
Crab-grass,
Dandelions,
Little children running and rolling in their Sunday best,
And peach festivals, though lately strawberries are the style.

. . .

"BEFORE THE ROPE BROKE, the cracked bell rang every Sunday,
Warming the hearts of all the few that made Bar Hallow
more than a B&O track, a post office, and a general store.
Common farmer men and women were proud of their
Church.
Devoted pastors came, preaching and praying,
Through depressions, repressions,
Broken windows and recessions.
White hair was respected, new ideas rejected.
Big families filled rough pews with children,
Who grew, matured, and became forgotten—
They were never known by the new who came,
Remembering only the places of their youth.

"BAR HALLOW HAD TO GROW—
Just as cities, cars, and cemented pavements squeezed
toward rural farms as for air.
The Church also grew to meet the need.
People loved her and did not have to be pandered into
her support.
They enlarged their Church and paid for it.
They were dedicated people."

"BUT—"
recovered the dazed Materialist.
His hands waved incessantly.
His voice boomed impressively.
"Everyone is crowded, chairs are in the aisles,
Our Children are not safe!
The Church must progress with the times.

People want conditioned air, cushioned chairs, bigger buildings,
A new efficient Church.
The carpet is bare—
The roof leaks—
The driveway is rutted.

"EVERYONE VOTED.
We leaders know what they want.
We must spend our monies on bricks and our energy attracting *new* Souls.
The *older* Members are set in their way and secure.
Everyone changes with the times.
Changes cost money."

"I KNOW THE PEOPLE ARE GIVING," cautioned the Spirit.
"I can feel their love everywhere.
Why are you selling my Church?"

"THE BEST WAY TO reach people is to advertise."
The Materialist was visibly impressing himself with his wit and intelligent answers.
"Any good business has a sales gimmick.
This year we are selling the Church back to the people.
They certainly cannot refuse."

THE MASTER SALESMAN nudged the Spirit in the ribs with his elbow,
Only to find the Spirit had no ribs.

Voices whispered throughout Eternity.
"Cheap...how cheap," whined many,
A braver spirit shouted—
"There is no room for God unless Love is free."
Materialism destroys God by merely existing.
It cannot hear even the loudest warning voice of Love.

"I PERSONALLY INVITE you to our groundbreaking,"
Tempted the Materialist.
"It will be a grand day for the greater Trinity."

"I SHALL NOT BE THERE," replied the Spirit.
My people will leave—slowly at first—but they will leave.
Many already have."
Looking down, the Spirit said goodbye to His Church.
A soft whisper echoed in the aged white building,
"Darkness is coming. *Watch out for our few.*"

EMERGENCY

Quiet and shadowy is the city at night. The streets and black alleys all have names, but these are meaningless symbols unless they mean home to some lonely soul. Under the dull lamplight, forms are strange and mysterious. Daylight shadows are welcome umbrellas from the heat of the sun, but night shadows strike ghoulish black and white fear. They are unknown quantities—dark, secretive places. The quiet, empty city is an immense naked giant.

Small sounds penetrate the night city. Harsh words shrill through steamed winter windows. A rat wants cheese. Snap goes the trap. A baby wakes—wails, moans, gurgles—and is again swallowed up in sleep. Sandpaper footsteps sound the path of the passing beat cop. An ugly gray dog with a frozen coat shivers in the gutter. His ears are long and his tail too short. He has no place in dog society. This matters not if one is a dog. Few look twice at a homely dog, but homely humans constantly gaze into mirrors, reminding themselves that they are ugly and out of place in their society. The nocturnal solitude is broken by the high rapid footsteps of a woman—hunched and afraid—going home. Under the corner post, she looks nervously from right to left, behind, and listens. Her worn heart is pounding faster than her crisp footsteps, walking, pausing, running. A door slams.

The city asleep at two o'clock in the morning is watched only by neon signs, sparse cops, empty hacks, and buzzing stoplights —blinking red, yellow, and green warnings to the empty black pitch of night. In their beds here sleep philosophers, poets, artists. Each man in slumber fancies himself a creator, though he be without a creation. Awake, these same men fear the black night of death and life.

A wailing white ambulance winds quickly through Columbus. Few sleepers stir at this common cry of a man in trouble. The white angle, turning from Main, roars along Seventh Street grinding to a halt in front of the lighted emergency entrance of Children's Hospital. The siren slows to an inaudible growl. Quickly, the driver and white attendant jump out and throw the rear door of the ambulance open. A stooped old doctor, holding a worn brown bag, helps the men carefully lift a white covered stretcher down the ramp toward the emergency room door.

～

I was slouching over a cup of black swamp root, as we benevolently called Ma Purkey's coffee in the hospital cafeteria. During my nightly graveyard shift at Kiddies, I enjoyed these moments of coffee and quiet conversation with the more interesting nursing students as they wandered in for stale sandwiches and coffee in Ma's kitchen. The faint chords of juked music and idle chatter were interrupted by the buzzing of the intercom.

"Mr. Barr is wanted in the Emergency Room!" Irma's bulky voice blasted throughout the building.

The hospital staff often contended that Irma, the telephone operator, did not need a public address system. If she belched, we would all run to the Emergency Room.

"I hope that you won't have to call me down." A red-eyed intern yawned between mouthfuls of soup.

"Nah! Some kid probably just crapped himself," I replied while grabbing a few slices of cold cuts and a waiting pot of coffee. I stopped to listen before leaving the room. The squawk box was again buzzing.

"Tell that old son of a Barr maiden not to forget my lunch!" Irma's detonating laughter followed me across the corridor and down two flights of stairs to the ER.

Reaching the emergency room, I pushed my way past chattering nurses and helpful bystanders. Irma's voice was echoing everywhere, paging doctors, superintendents, nurses, and oxygen therapists. Rushing half-dressed professional forms, smelling of nicotine and coffee, assumed a quiet dignity in the chaos of performing their particular duties. Children's Hospital quickly became an organized unit—ready for an emergency.

As I neared my desk as clerk of admissions, I caught snatches of varied conversations in many moods and voices.

"Sled riding after dark—bad accident?—two hour ride to the hospital—Oh! What a shame. Such a big boy and only fifteen— ambulance skidded and hit a car—Nurse! Get me a cut down tray—Dr. Isaac Black!—Look at that blood on the floor, Mommy!—Dr. Isaac Black!—Quiet, dear."

"Bill, get these papers signed so we can start to work on him. He can't last without a transfusion!"

A surgeon's intern angled me toward the gray old doctor who was standing alone and out of the way. The distinguished old man had the pensively sorrowful look of a man feeling useless and out of place in a modern hospital.

In a matter-of-fact, quiet tone, the old man began to automatically give me the boy's vital statistics as we moved toward the stretcher at the middle of the room. The boy had gone bobsledding with a group of his teenage friends. The sled had struck a log. He fell off, but before he could roll away, the machine had run over him. One of the sled runners had smashed into the side of his face.

The doctor took a faded yellow handkerchief from his vest and wiped the steam from his wire-framed glasses. "It took us two hours to drive here. The ambulance was involved in a minor accident. The roads were bad."

Before I could move to speak, the doctor reached for my pad.

"I have the mother's written permission. I'll sign for the boy." He nervously scrawled his name across the blue sheet. *Frederick Donald Brown, M.D.*

Quickly, I typed a name tag for Don Blake and walked to the young boy who was writhing and gurgling from a pain no sedative could conquer. The suffocating mixture of alcohol and ether was making my eyes misty and my head light.

"His lungs are filling up. Call Doctor Smith!" a deep voice was saying with calm authority.

Irma's voice again broke through the heavy air.

After tapping the surgeon gently on his shoulder to announce my presence, I began to fashion an armband on the boy's massive wrist.

He was the largest boy I had ever seen at Children's Hospital. Don Blake was a massive frame of bones—only fifteen and already six feet tall. His crewed blond hair was matted with blood. Pink brain meat was visible through the wide slash on the side of his skull. One of his blinded eyes, hanging by a nerve thread, was clinging to his peach smooth chin. His other eye was bulged and bloated shut, its purple veins dilated and broken from the grimacing pain. Three bloody teeth were pushed back at an odd angle toward the roof of his open mouth. The boy was no longer bleeding, except for the small stream of red spittle that flowed down his chin with every breath.

I returned to my desk and began the endless paperwork of

admitting a patient to Children's Hospital. Across from my desk, the old doctor was sitting, the ancient brown medical bag on his lap.

"I prefer to spend my time waiting down here with all the noise," the old man said. "May I smoke?"

I offered a wrinkled pack of Luckies, but the old man waved me away with a grin and reached into his vest for an ancient brown pipe. Striking a wooden match on the edge of my desk, drawing a few slow puffs of black smoke, he began to send clouds of contented aroma throughout the small cubicle that was my office.

I first broke the silence.

"I can't understand why the young and healthy must have accidents and suffer pain. Upstairs is a boy with part of his backbone missing. He has lived for years, a mass of jelly and bones that will never be able to support their own weight." I pulled a yellow card from the large file on my desk. "Here is a child who has been here for two weeks. She was born without bones in her arms and legs. These children, who will never be normal, are living on and on, while a healthy Adonis like Don Blake is fighting for his very last breath. Doctor! It does not make sense!"

The old man rubbed his nose nervously and began to talk. "Son"—his voice broke slightly—"you have not been around death long enough to understand the way of God. One cannot be sentimental where life and death are concerned. Death is real —cold and hard. I've sat these night vigils for more years than you have lived. I know men. They fear life as much as they fear death. During the day, they fear the faces and forms they can see. At night, they fear the shadows they cannot recognize."

The long night passed quickly as I listened to and learned to love the old doctor's philosophy. The telephone interrupted us. On a pad, I scratched a note to post in the morning journal:

Donald Blake, 15. Expired, 5:45 am. Children's.

I did not say a word. Somehow, the old man sensed what had happened. Hospital scuttlebutt says that old doctors know death too well. The doctor pulled on his coat and walked out.

Good morning, sir!

The words never came out. They remained locked in my throat.

Outside, the gray dawn sky was chasing the night shadows away—creating fresh patterns of light and shadow.

The city was awakening to a new day of living and dying and being afraid.

THE CROWD AT THE CORNER

There is a crowd at the corner.

On a summer's June afternoon, only humans can be found on a red brick city street. Stray mongrels are all in their solitary cool places, scratching fleas and dreaming dreams of the coming beclouded night hours. Occasionally, an automobile roars past, bestrewing its gaseous cloud behind to mingle with the astute stench of steaming sidewalks, stale coffee, dirty children, and filthy garbage cans. Long rows of tall, broken buildings decorate the narrow red street. A few flower boxes spot the tired buildings with color, breaking the monotonous pattern of dusty screened windows. Buildings bake and sidewalks crack in the heat of the summer sun.

A thin brown child, clad only in shorts, is making animal sounds and pedaling her tricycle in a wide circle over the dusty street that is her playground. One of the worn thin wheels of her rusting toy becomes stuck fast in a crack between the bricks. Climbing down from her position as truck driver, the lonely tomboy becomes a mechanic. Impatient hands claw and tug at the stuck wheel. It will not budge. Whimpering softly, the brown mechanic becomes a little girl again. Unattended, she is left crying in the street. Her mother is down at the corner.

On a narrow board swaying high above the street, a man is standing and sweating. He is gray and thin—much too frail to be up so high. He is a painter. The steady swish and slap of his brush cannot be heard on the street. The only indications of his presence are the white spotted drippings on the windows and sidewalks below. His life has been spent at the narcotic monotony of scrapping the weathered and placing a cheerful façade on decaying wood. The leather-baked rind of his face shows the sacred sensitivity of age. He automatically dips the wet brush into the swinging pail at his side. Eight hours each day his brush slaps—throughout the cool morning and hot afternoon. His alert and active mind escapes the tedium of the moment by returning and reliving green youthful country scenes and pondering the future his pension will bring.

"Too bad Mag is gone." The sound gurgles harshly in his dry throat.

The old man does not know he is talking. He sees only the soft sod of a new grave covering the only life he loved. Clinging high and forgotten to the side of a building, the old man often releases his mental burden by talking to God and the angels he sees around him. Setting brush and pail on the narrow board, the old painter pulls a railroad handkerchief from his pocket and wipes the sweaty tears from his eyes.

A shrill bell is ringing on the street. Shaded from the heat by a wide faded umbrella, a short squatty man struggles to move his yellow high-wheeled cart over the rough pavement. The jolly red-faced ice cream man is singing loudly the Italian Street Song. Last night during the dark hours he had the satisfaction of knowing that snug children were dreaming in anticipation of this daily visit. Each day his brisk bell sounds a ritual celebration on the street. Eager half-dressed children dash and pounce on him, shoving fistfuls of pennies into his apron to be exchanged for chocolate-covered ice cream bars. For an instant, Old Nick is king, even though he drags one foot. The happy children daily give him courage to return to the streets and the staring people. Nick feels worthwhile as he listens to the laughing children and watches them run and perform the many childish games he could never play. After hogging down every last bit of the precious ice cream, the children teach the old cripple to laugh and love living. Chewing their sticks, they march after their limping friend, padding the street with their many naked feet. Old Nick is lucky. Loneliness has never bothered him since he began his pushcart business.

When he notices the little brown girl crying, Old Nick's robust smile turns to one of pensive concern. Bracing his useless leg against the cart, he lifts the tiny child from the street. Her small fingers claw for the large stick of ice cream he holds high above her reach. The rain clouds disappear, and the sun again begins to radiate in the child's large brown eyes. Without a spoken word, she becomes Nick's own child. Happily ladylike, she begins to tell her friend the story of her unladylike distress. Reaching down, Nick frees the cycle from the rut, but he cannot keep from wondering where the other children are and why this girl is alone in the street.

The little girl leading the way, Nick hobbles toward the growing crowd at the corner. Being short as well as round, Nick cannot see over the housewives and idle men that form the crowd.

A bald man is fanning the flies with a folded newspaper and smoking. A square-jawed lady with blue hair is slowly grinding her chewing gum. Her periodic laughter is ancient and rusty. A young man with hands in his pockets is squashing a loaf of bread under his arm. Children standing on one foot and then the other sway as they clutch their mothers' skirts. Only the muffled wail of a baby breaks the silence. Not one has a word of greeting for the other. This crowd of pushing people are merely here to witness another of the small dramas of the street.

No one makes a move to help Crazy Ruth or her son.

The boy is lying on the broken sidewalk, shaking and biting his tongue. His eyes are bulging from their sockets. Pain has contorted his face into the ghoulish stare of an idiot boy. It has all happened before. Crazy Ruth, the scrubwoman, and her feeble son are known on the street. Standing strangely majestic in the center of the crowd, she holds tightly with her bony white fingers the hand of the writhing boy. Ruth looks heavy and hot. She always wears a lint-covered black sweater to cover the tears in her faded sack-like garment. She is oblivious of the crowd, and her eyes silently plead from the bottom of a soul that can no longer cry that her boy will soon get up and follow her home.

Not one person thinks of helping the weary white old lady. Their eyes are glued on the boy. He can only return his mother's love by scratching and clawing at the red street. A score of hands are within reach of the pitiful woman, but she is more alone than the painter high on the side of an adjacent building.

Equally unnoticed is the blue protector of the people who appears behind the awed crowd.

"Go home, you people!" His blasting voice startles the indolent circle of spectators.

Sluggishly, they begin to plod away, whispering and casting furtive glances at the mournful old lady and her son. The hollow tapping sound of his night stick grows faints as the policeman walks down the block.

Old Nick is limping after the young thieves that have stolen his cart. The little brown girl is pedaling a new circle over the rough bricks of the street. Slamming screen doors penetrate the sticky June day. It is noon, and the painter is climbing down for lunch.

On the street, life is continuing. Lonely people, caught in the human trap, remain lost within themselves.

It is only a woman down at the corner.

She has an idiot son.

SERMONS

THANKING GOD ALWAYS

Avowing His Love
    Appreciating His Gifts
    Awaiting His Return

Trinity Lutheran Church, Galion, Ohio
    October 13, 1963
    Trinity XVIII

TEXT: 1 Corinthians 1:4-9
    I AM ALWAYS thanking God for you. I thank him for his
grace given to you in Christ Jesus. I thank him for all the enrich-
ment that has come to you in Christ. You possess full knowledge
and you can give full expression to it, because in you the
evidence for the truth of Christ has found confirmation. There is
indeed no single gift you lack, while you wait expectantly for
our Lord Jesus Christ to reveal himself. He will keep you firm to
the end, without reproach on the Day of our Lord Jesus. It is
God himself who called you to share in the life of his Son Jesus
Christ our Lord; and God keeps faith.
    IT SEEMS TO BE the general belief that the will of God is to

make things distasteful for us—like taking bad-tasting medicine when we are sick, or going to the dentist.

SOMEBODY NEEDS TO TELL US that the sunrise is also God's will. This is the time of harvest, the harvest that will provide food and clothing for us without which we could not live on earth.

GOD ORDERED THE SEASONS. They are his will. In fact, the good things in life far outweigh the bad. There are more sunrises than cyclones. There are more tomorrows than tornadoes.

IT IS EASY to thank God when we see his warmth and good-ness springing from a full golden ear of corn, when we see our freezers stocked in the basement, pumpkin pie on the table. But we should not thank God only during one season of the year. WE SHOULD THANK GOD ALWAYS, by avowing his love, appreciating his gifts, and awaiting his return.

BUT FROM CHILDHOOD until the hour we draw our last breath, one of the worst enemies of our health and well-being, and of our ability to contribute to the health and well-being of others, is the temptation to think only of ourselves, to worship ourselves, to pity ourselves.

SURELY THE WORM OF SELF-PITY is one of the worst pests in the garden of our lives. How often we say by our atti-tudes, "I feel so sorry for myself. I really am a fine person, admirable and lovable. But few people really appreciate me for what I am or realize what a hard time I am having. Everything is wrong. Poor me!"

WE CAN at times understand the little ditty sung by children:

Nobody loves me. Everybody hates me,
I'm going to eat some worms.
Big, fat, juicy worms.

SOME TIME AGO in a popular musical comedy, a weak and susceptible woman explaining to the audience why she unfailingly succumbed to temptation sang out, "How can I be what I ain't?" Far from comedy, this is one of the most tragic questions persistently aske. "How can I be anything else? I'm set in my ways! What chance is there of making a change?"

THERE IS AN ANSWER to these questions, and Christianity has it. Paul puts it this way, "It is God Himself who called you to share in the life of his Son Jesus Christ our Lord; and God keeps faith." That is the essence of the glad Christian gospel. You don't need to stay the way you are. To find Christ and to tell others of him in thankful lives is the answer.

IS THERE ANY real joy in the world now that the Lord has come? Comedians may be the highest-paid people in the world today, but real joy is richer and deeper than wisecracks from a TV screen or a radio loudspeaker. How often we are reminded today of the "high cost of living."

THOSE WHO HAVE LET the Lord Jesus Christ command their lives share in the joy of the victory of the empty tomb. At the sacrifice of his life, Christ has brought us the favor of God. We who share in his spirit receive his favor. He loves us. He understands our problems. He bears us good will. He bestows on us fatherly smiles and blessings.

IT IS A HIGH AND NOBLE thing when we place ourselves in the background and thank God for blessing us and our friends. We show our true affection for friends by praying for them. As Paul thanked God for his friends in the Corinthian Church, so should we thank God always for the gifts, graces, and comforts we have been given in this church.

THE CONGREGATION AT CORINTH appreciated all of the gifts that God had given them. They gave of themselves. They became servants of the servants of God. Paul could always depend on them to labor the extra mile with him. And because they were willing to move ahead and serve, they stood out among the early Christian churches as a congregation that was blessed.

THIS CONGREGATION has been richly blessed. Trinity Church has come a long way since the days when your husbands and fathers—and many of you sitting here this morning—carried water, wood, and cement and pieced together this building brick by brick, stone by stone, in an act of faith. Those were the days when men and women here had enough faith that they would work for forty cents an hour and give twenty cents back to the church.

AND THEY BUILT THIS CHURCH with their own hands— not for their own good, but for the good of Galion and for the good of the Kingdom of God. We thank God for the heritage these men and women of faith have given us, and the rich blessings that we have received as a result of their labor.

IN HONOR of their faith, we must continue in the good work they started. We cannot live the rest of our lives sitting in the shadow of what they have done. God gave them courage to begin. Now, God will give us courage to move on.

WE APPRECIATE BLESSINGS most when others share in them. We have something to offer the lost and lonely of this city. We have been touched here by the Spirit of Christ and, through us, this city can be touched by his love and power.

HOW DOES THIS HAPPEN?

WHEN CHRIS RESINER was pastor of a large congregation in New York City, he sent out an invitation to the street sweepers of the city, asking them to be guests at an evening service. Nearly five hundred of them came, wearing the white suits—the uniforms they wore when they swept the streets.

Dr. Reisner said, "I preached to them. They were the lowliest of the lowly in our city, and I preached to them that God saw in them the elements of divinity that made them men."

That night, one old man with a foreign accent rose and said, "Dr. Reisner, will you permit me to say a word on behalf of these men? We are extremely grateful to you for inviting us here tonight. We have swept the streets of New York for years. I myself have been a street sweeper for twenty-five years, and this is the first time in the twenty-five years that anybody in this city has ever paid any attention to us. I am going to go back tomorrow and sweep the streets of this town with a little more care because somebody saw in me a man worth inviting to church."

THERE ARE HUNDREDS in this city who are waiting for your invitation to come and serve God with you here.

WE OUGHT TO BE THANKFUL that, because of the death of Jesus Christ, we are somebody. Trinity Congregation is somebody. No matter what, we are called to do this in life. No matter whether we are called to preach Christ, plant corn, drive a truck, or raise a family, we are all called to touch others with the love of Christ.

AS A CHRISTIAN CONGREGATION, we are awaiting Christ's return. We do not know the hour or the day, but we do know that he is coming. He is going to ask each one of us, "What have you done for my Church?"

I NOTICE A FEAR of change here, a reluctance to accept God's blessings and move forward.

JOHNSTOWN, PENNSYLVANIA had an air of fear and dread a few years ago. The engineers said the great dam that had stood for so many years was going to break in a few hours.

THE RAIN had been falling for days. The water had backed up. When the engineers found a little crack in the dam, they said, "Flee to the hills. Go to the mountains. The flood is coming!"

BUT THERE WERE hundreds of people who said, "Why,

those young college students don't know what they're talking about! That dam has stood for years."

THEY STAYED in their places of business and in their homes. Suddenly, there was a crash and a roar, and down the valley, millions and millions of gallons of water rushed to sweep 2,300 people to their deaths because they refused to be warned and refused to move.

I TELL YOU, God has been faithful to us here. He has come again and again with uncountable blessings. So should we be faithful to him, by moving at his command and living our lives for him—by THANKING HIM ALWAYS.

AMEN.

LOOK TO THE WILL OF CHRIST

Looking Up To His Wisdom
    Looking Out To His Work
    Looking Forward To His Way

Trinity Lutheran Church, Galion, Ohio
    October 27, 1963
    Trinity XX
    Reformation Sunday

TEXT: Ephesians 5:15-21. NEB.

BE MOST CAREFUL then how you conduct yourselves: like sensible people, not like simpletons. Use the present opportunity to the full, for these are evil days. So do not be fools, but try to understand what the will of the Lord is. Do not give way to drunkenness and the dissipation that goes with it, but let the Holy Spirit fill you: speak to one another in psalms, hymns, and songs; sing and make music in your hearts to the Lord; and in the name of our Lord Jesus Christ, give thanks every day for everything to our God and Creator. Be subject to one another out of reverence for Christ.

THE HOSPITAL CHAPLAIN leaned gently over the bed of the pathetic little guy whose attempt at suicide had missed its mark.

"WHY DID YOU DO IT, ALF?" he whispered.

ACCUSATION stood strong in Alf's tired eyes, but his voice held only a weak wisp of sound. "It wasn't no use goin' on. There ain't no good news left in the world today. If there was, somebody would have come runnin' with it!"

AN ABANDONED FORSAKEDNESS haunted the little guy's hopeless words. Those words probe deeply into the heart of our bewildered generation. Was Alf right? Are we really forsaken? Is there any good news left in the world today? If so, what is it? And why aren't we better equipped to come running with it?"

SECONDARY GOALS have nudged us away from the high destiny for which we were created by God who loved the world. We fight as drowning men and women flailing for air, man and women completely forsaken, completely cut off and abandoned by all that is right and good.

THIS LOSS OF PROPORTION and purpose is everywhere around us. Consider this advertisement a school of music inserted not long ago in a Columbus newspaper. "Start your child on the violin," the headline urged. Then followed three featured reasons for having your child learn to play the instrument of Stradivarius:

To improve his posture.

To train his memory

To coordinate his mental faculties.

THERE WAS NOT a syllable about studying the violin to create the sound of music. That's like having a woman take piano lessons for the chief purpose of achieving shorter fingernails! Or a boxer faithfully taking organ lessons because the pedals of the console will help him achieve more nimble footwork!

NOW, there's nothing wrong with improving posture or training memories or coordinating mental faculties—or even with having shorter fingernails or more agile legs. But these ends are worlds removed from the vision of a loving God putting it into the hearts of His Children to build instruments and to compose music. In short, this ad is wrong simply because it chooses a wrong goal and thus asks us to expect the wrong result.

UNDER THE mounting pressures of this fretful and frazzled age, we have largely lost our sense of proportion. We've forgotten to put first things first. A dictator's shoe banging against a tabletop sounds to us like all the fury of an exploding atomic bomb. It is in a nervous time like today that we must look to the will of Christ by looking up to His wisdom, looking out to His work, and looking forward to His way.

WE LOOK UP to the wisdom of Christ by wishing to know God better. Christ desires that we know God. Christ's Spirit is here! No one can deny that Jesus Christ is truly here in this sanctuary this morning, touching us with God's love and wisdom.

WE HAVE SEEN IT over and over throughout history how, when the church fell into error and disgrace, Christ has repeatedly returned and lifted God's church up.

THAT'S WHAT HAPPENED in the sixteenth century when the church turned its face away from God and stepped into the shadow of darkness and despair, working with the Devil while pretending to build monuments of stone to God. Then God spoke through Martin Luther who, through pain and sacrifice, stood with Christ and shouted to a sin-blackened world, "Here I stand!" And standing there with Christ, he prevailed and the church marched on.

WHERE DO YOU STAND TODAY?

IF WE ARE TO KNOW the wisdom of Christ in our lives, Christ demands that we stand with God and walk exactly according to God's will. If we are to walk according to God's will, we must open our ears and listen and be attentive to what God's will is. We must stop playing at religion and start *doing* religion. We have kept Christ in the past tense long enough. What we need today is a religion at work *now*. Today calls for a present tense religion.

A HUMOROUS STORY is told of a teacher who was instructing her children in school regarding verb tense.

SHE SAID, "Now, children, if I say, I was beautiful, that is past tense. If I say, I will be beautiful, that is future tense. But if I say, I am beautiful, what is that?"

A LITTLE BOY in the front row answered, "That's pretense!"

IT IS A PRESENT TENSE religion we need today, not pretense. We must forget ourselves—what we are—and look to Christ and find out what God is and what God's will is for our lives.

HOW ELSE can it be and still lead to maturity? If we were not constantly growing souls, we'd be vacuum-packed puppets jerked on senseless strings. When the awful gauntlet of human tragedy is thrown down before us, we don't turn for comfort to the twisting teenager, to LSD or pot, or to the selfish cynic that finds all of life meaningless. Rather, we turn to Christ—that soul who has stood unforgettably on the thin edge of his own valley of the shadow, wrestling with his problem in dark agony, and not deserting the fight until by the grace of God he battles His way back in triumph!

IT IS THE WILL of Christ that we look out for God's work in this world. God has given us everything that we have not because we deserve it, but because God loves us, God longs for us, and God lives again for us.

THAT IS WHAT ENCOUNTER IS ALL ABOUT!

WE WHO RECOGNIZE God's grace must redeem God's time in this world. We live in a world that is close to death, in a world where time is running out. It is Christ's will that we regain the lost, that we save what we can of what is left. There is something for each one of us to do, and we must make use of the time that has been given us. We must guard against losing what time we have by thinking of ourselves and being depressed, discouraged, and disillusioned.

LIVING OUR LIVES at the delicate edge of eternity, we must keep all of our senses awake to human need by bringing that human need to the Lord every day in a dedicated life of prayer.

ONE OF the great business leaders of our time is J. Arthur Rank. He has an elevator straight up to his office, but he does not use it. He prefers the stairs. He calls them his "prayer stairs." In the morning, as he walked up, he prays, asking God to guide him in every step he takes that day.

AS HE TAKES each step separately and deliberately, he prays! He finally arrives at the top—at the top in more ways than one—at the top looking out for the work of Christ in this world.

WHEN WE LOOK to the wisdom of Christ, and when we look out for the work of Christ, only then can we look forward to God's way.

ARE YOU DOING ANYTHING? Is your life really counting for something important? Are you in this game of life honestly and sincerely? Or does it seem to you that you are placing the emphasis on the wrong things—that you are just here, riding along day after day, waiting to do something someday, somehow when the time is ripe, when you get the breaks?

WELL! NOW IS THE TIME! Today calls for forthright doers of God's Word and Will. God is standing by to help us, but time is running out!

WALTER RUSSELL HOWIE once wrote a parable to illustrate this point. It concerns a man lying critically ill. On one side of his bed, a nurse is bustling, and on the other side, the doctor is bending over attentively. And because angels are involved in this parable, the following conversation was heard by neither doctor nor nurse.

The dying man's Guardian Angel whispered to him, "Are you ready to go?"

The man roused himself sufficiently to answer, "Certainly, I' ready. I cut quite a swathe through life and got lots of important things done. Sure. Let's go!"

But the Recording Angel, looking down from Peter's gate, said to the Guardian Angel, "But his hands are dirty."

"Yes," the Guardian admitted, "He did sometimes dabble in those things in life which soil the hands and besmudge the heart."

"Furthermore," continued the Recorder, "his boots are all muddy."

"Yes, he sometimes took a shortcut through the muck to avoid going the long way around where his quiet duty lay. He was quite a busy man, you see, dealing in the big issues, and often he felt he had to cut corners."

"And his clothing," said the Angel of the Records. "It's torn and bloodstained."

"Yes," said the Guardian Angel sadly. "He fought with his brother."

At this point in the conversation, the man objected indignantly, "But I have no brother!"

"You see," said the Recording Angel, "he doesn't even know he has many brothers!"

Then the angel looked down at the man and whispered softly, "Would you like to go back and try once more? I've left the door of life open for you."

kAt that juncture, the physician straightened up and said quietly to the nurse, "The crisis is past. He will live."

BECAUSE OF JESUS CHRIST, our crisis is past. Will we live?

STEPPING FORWARD WITH CHRIST

Trinity Lutheran Church, Galion Ohio
   November 3, 1963
   Trinity XXI
   On Occasion of Introduction of New Hymnal

TEXT: Psalm 96: 1-6.

O SING TO THE LORD a new song; sing to the Lord, all the earth! Sing to the Lord, bless his name; tell of his salvation from day to day. Declare his glory among the nations, his marvelous works among all the peoples! For great is the Lord, and greatly to be praised; he is to be feared above all gods. For all the gods of the peoples are idols; but the Lord made the heavens. Honor and majesty are before him; strength and beauty are in his sanctuary.

NOT LONG AGO an old tri-motor Ford airplane named the "Tin Goose" took off from the Los Angeles International Airport on a transcontinental flight. It was loaded with eager passengers who wished to reenact the commercial airline travel of thirty years ago.

THE OLD PLANE sputtered and coughed into life. Its

exhaust flamed out clouds of black carbon into the early morning darkness. Slowly, the cumbersome plane taxied to the edge of the runway. There, the old bird stood poised, shaking and screaming, waiting for flight. The plane slowly shuttered down the runway—and after what seemed too long a time, groaned into the air, rose, and disappeared into the clouds.

THIRTY YEARS AGO, when the "Tin Goose" was in her heyday, flying was a risk and an adventure. Those hearty passengers who dared took off from Newark, New Jersey—flew in one day to Kansas City—stayed there overnight—and if the plane was on schedule, they arrived the next evening in Los Angeles. Forty-eight hours—cramped and crowded.

TODAY the same distance can be covered by a modern jetliner in four hours and fifty-five minutes! Passengers are no longer jolted and tossed by low altitude wind currents in a plane that flew at some three- to five-thousand feet.

THE GIANT AIRCRAFT of today soar above the turbulence and storms—out beyond the clouds—higher than the wind—at thirty to thirty-five thousand feet—at speeds up to 650 miles an hour. The passenger of today rides in noiseless "vibration-free" luxury, in comfort, security, and safety.

ALL OF THESE ADVANCES in air travel have occurred in our lifetime. Most of them have occurred in my brief span of years. There is not one here this morning who can predict the speed and comfort of the planes—or rockets—we will have a decade from now!

ALONG WITH these marvels of transportation have come a uniting of the people of the globe through instant communication and air travel.

STUDENTS can today rove to the far corners of the earth to learn how other people live and think. Medicines and doctors and nurses are rushed to epidemic-stricken areas while they can still do some good and save lives. Missionaries penetrate the most primitive regions quickly and effectively. The Bible can be flown to any part of the world in a matter of a few hours.

FOR GOOD WILL as well as for war, the airplane has progressed to become a winged instrument of men stepping forward with Christ. The airplane has helped "Declare God's glory among the nations, His marvelous works among all peoples!"

AFTER SOME FORTY HOURS of laboring across the continent, the old "Tin Goose" nosed down into the Washington Airport and coughed to a stop. Somewhat shaken, streaked with dirt from the long hot ride in an over-heated cabin, but still smiling, the group of reporters and executives left the ancient airplane—glad that their sentimental journey was over.

NOT ONE OF THOSE PASSENGERS said: "Let's go back to the airplanes they had when I was a boy!" Instead they consigned the "Tin Goose" to the museum where she belonged and took the jet back to Los Angeles!

THEY WOULDN'T THINK of going back to the crude airplane of thirty years ago. Just as we wouldn't think of going back to the kerosene lamp, the wood stove, the Model A Ford, or the outhouse in the backyard—although we may dream of "the good old days." The Good Old Days! The good old days were good—but not as good as good old today!

AS WE progress through life, changes come often, and they often come hard.

IT IS DIFFICULT to make any change, even when making it as missionaries for Jesus Christ. You all know how hard it is for a young child to stand on his own two feet and take his first step. He struggles and shakes at the weight of his own body. He wants to walk, but it seems only natural to remain crawling on all fours. To take the first step is a real challenge.

I CAN REMEMBER how difficult it was for me to stay out

alone all night in my backyard tent for the first time. It was a change in my life.

THERE WAS A BRIGHT MOON, and my old dog was right there in the sleeping bag with me with all of his burrs and fleas. But it was all that I could do to keep myself from running back into the house to my freshly turned down bed and pull the covers tightly over my head and shut out all of my fears of the dark unknown—like an ostrich burying its head in the sand. We are only human and are tempted to run back to the things we know best.

IT WAS DIFFICULT FOR ME to leave my family and friends and go to the university. I saw tears fill my mother's eyes as she drove away, leaving her solitary son alone in the big city for the first time in his life. She knew I would never be the same again. I would be better—but somehow, not the same. As the years went on, she learned to love me for what I am and not for what I was.

IT WAS DIFFICULT for me to change my whole life and come to Galion—and face a congregation of sensitive and lovely people who were discouraged, distrustful, and angry with God and with each other.

I AM LIKE YOU! I am afraid of any change until I take that first step into the unknown. But I have no fear when I step out with Christ! His love holds me up and gives me the courage to go on. He provides the challenge. He helps me to look at people and life as they really are—not with soap-opera sentimentality —not shrouding the future with the veil of the past. But seeking the future with the whole heart—seeing our security in Christ.

NEXT WEEK, Trinity Congregation is going to make a change. When we begin to use the new hymnal we have purchased—with its beautiful liturgy—our services will never be the same again. They will be better—but they will somehow never be the same again. Scholarship in the church has never stopped throughout the centuries. Changes are inevitable if there is to be progress in Christian worship. We are here to serve Christ and that calls for a "daily renewal" or a "daily change" if we are to bring His salvation into a disturbed, decayed, and dying world.

THIS CHANGE will be a test of our faith—to see whether the form of our worship will come between us and the Christ we adore and serve.

IT WILL BE A CHALLENGE every step of the way! It will be difficult for a while, but it won't be difficult forever. We are not stepping out into an unknown. We are stepping out with Christ into eternal joy and happiness. This is His promise. To step out and move forward with Him is our duty!

For—

The peace of God is for those who obey;
Who listen and hear his voice each day,
Who listen and march by the Master's side,
Who have heard the call and have not denied.

The man who will know the peace of God,
Is the man who will walk where the Master trod.

AMEN.

IMITATORS OF CHRIST

Trinity Lutheran Church, Galion, Ohio
  November 17, 1963
  Trinity XXIII

TEXT: Philippians 3:17-21

BRETHREN, join in imitating me, and mark those who so live as you have an example in us. For many, of whom I have often told you and now tell you even with tears, live as enemies of the cross of Christ. Their end is destruction, their god is the belly, and they glory in their shame, with minds set on earthly things. But our commonwealth is in heaven, and from it, we await a Savior, the Lord Jesus Christ, who will change our lowly body to be like his glorious body, by the power which enables him even to subject all things to himself.

ELEVEN CENTS does not mean very much anymore—does it? A dime and a penny—that is all eleven cents is! A dime will not take you far, and a penny is hardly worth mentioning.

IN MY WALLET, I have carried a letter written on March 6, 1955 by a woman that I have never met. This torn and ragged letter was written to me when I was manager of the student snack bar at Capital University. As you can see, the paper is brown with age and bent and torn from being carried with all of the charge-a-plates and credit cards that seem to be necessary in our modern society. The letter comes from Laurelville, Ohio. I would like to share it with you.

"KIND SIR:" (the lady writes) "Please accept the contents of this letter. You may think it foolish, but I have to do it to be clear with my own heart and God.

"A week ago Tuesday, we were up to the concert at your school and my little boy bought a sandwich in the restaurant and gave them a dollar and they gave him back 91 cents. So I figured they gave him 11 cents too much money.

"We are Christians and are trying to keep straight. So I feel like I should do this as it is my responsibility to my child to imitate God. We must keep our slate clean. I don't want anything to stand between me when I face Him—do you?

"Here is the 11 cents." –Sincerely, Mrs. Aldena Slager.

A DIME AND A PENNY fell out of the envelope onto the lunch counter. I could not help but weep as I rang 11 cents on the cash register and dropped the small coins in the drawer. Here was a lady who, out of concern for her child and her own soul, really knew how to imitate Christ. Eleven cents worth of her good work seems like small change by comparison.

I HAVE READ this letter to people many times since 1955. And every time that I have read it, it has been laughed at and considered foolish.

"IT COST that old girl four cents to send back eleven," someone once told me.

"SHE IS A FOOL!" a friend of mine remarked. "That Snack Bar has bled us dry for years. It's good to see them bleed once in a while."

A BOY WHO WAS STUDYING for the ministry quipped, "I

don't like people who parade around their religion like that woman!"

IN ALL OF the discussions that I have had over this aged piece of paper, not one person has noticed that the real issue here is not "eleven cents," but the fact that here we come face to face with a Christian who sees it as her Christian duty to imitate Christ in her everyday life.

ELEVEN CENTS will not make or break any one of us, but how well we imitate Christ can spell the success or failure of our Christian lives.

CHRISTIAN VALUES have largely been lost in the world in which we live. Those who faithfully try to imitate Christ in their daily lives are quickly labeled as DOWNRIGHT FOOLS! When we find fifty-cents in the coin release of a public telephone, we would be called foolish if we dialed the operator and asked her to take the fifty-cents back. How many of you, if the candy machine gave you four bars for a nickel, would give three back? If the parking meter won't take your penny, do you leave it on top?

A FEW WEEKS AGO, I was invited to give the invocation at the annual seminar of the Real Estate Board of Galion, held at the Ritchie House. In my prayer, I thanked God for calling us to the work that we do, whether we preach Christ, plant corn, or buy and sell those things that he has given us.

WHEN THE DINNER was over, the President of the Ohio Association of Realtors stood up to speak on "The Ethics of Real Estate." After introducing his topic, he looked straight at me and said, "This is the first time I ever heard that selling real estate is a calling from God

THEN he got that certain smile on his face and said, "We realtors believe in the golden rule. Do to others as you would have them do to you!" Everybody laughed. They, too, thought it foolish to think that God had anything to do with the business world.

IN THE SPIRIT OF OUR TEST, Paul says: "Join with me in imitating Christ!" To imitate Christ means to be exactly like Jesus. Jesus looked foolish to the world of his day. We will appear foolish if we truly imitate Jesus today!

THIS IS A WORLD of astronauts and countdowns and blastoffs—a world of vitamins and cholesterol and Salk vaccines. There does not seem to be room for Jesus anymore. This is a hard world in which we live—a hard world peopled by magnanimous Abrahams and greedy Lots, by cunning Jacobs and transparent Josephs, by moody Elijahs, by hot-blooded Davids, treacherous Jezebels, and adventuresome Pauls.

WITH OUR NOBLE EYE, we view the worst of them and are obliged to say, "There but for the grace of God go I!"

INSTEAD of becoming imitators of Christ, we are too often satisfied to be only "mimics" of Christ. Instead of becoming exactly like him, we pretend to be like Jesus.

CHRISTIAN MIMICS look good enough to get by. They look good enough to be believable. At least they look good enough to get praises from the world. Like the true mimic, we often put on a cheerful false face while we scowl, grumble, murmur, and complain. We look good, but we don't do good!

YOU SEE, a mimic has everything on his own terms. He decides what he is going to do, when he is going to do it, and how it is going to be done. A mimic turns on his goodness to suit the occasion, or more often to suit himself. Night at bars, and then come to church the next morning.

THE CHRISTIAN who wants to do good, but only on his own terms no matter what anyone else thinks, is not an imitator of Christ. He's only a mimic.

WITH TEARS IN HIS EYES, Paul calls these "mimic Christians" enemies of the cross of Christ. Paul goes on to tell us,

"Their end is destruction! Their God is the belly! And they glory in their shame with their minds yet on earthly things."

WHEN A YOUNG CHILD pretends to be somebody or to do something, it is just a game and nobody gets hurt. But our Christian lives are not a game. The world is not our playground. If we fail at this job of imitating Christ—or of becoming exactly like Christ—WE WILL BE DESTROYED.

HENRICK IBSEN'S *PEER GYNT* is perhaps literature's best portrayal of the self-centered hell that all of us have experienced to some degree when we demand that everything be done our way, regardless of the cost to others. From the moment he abandoned his young love to get what he thought he wanted, he found himself more and more frustrated. He traveled all over the world trying to find himself. The further he went, the more sure he became that all things conspired to bring him to misery.

AT LAST in a hotel in Cairo, Egypt, he was confronted by a distinguished-looking gentleman who bowed sharply, saluted him, and called him "Emperor." "At last," thought Peer Gynt, "I am being recognized for what I am!" With new hope, he followed the man, only to find himself in an insane asylum. Every man in that dreadful place was an Emperor. Most of them thought they were Napoleon.

TO BE CENTERED in ourselves to the point that we forget about the Lord's will is truly the one great insanity! Not only in mental hospitals are the victims of this kind of madness found, but in many hours in the lives of all of us. Self-centeredness makes the work of the church impossible. Somehow, we must get out of the cask of self.

TO IMITATE CHRIST means to do Christ's work. Our church has been richly blessed in past weeks. I feel our Spirit of Christ here, and it is real, not a mimic. Have you noticed how good our choir has been sounding lately? They have learned to love the Lord and each other. To sing God's praise has become a joy. In our congregation, everybody wants to do something. Prayers are being asked for the sick, and the sick are getting well. Baskets of food have been taken to the poor from the canned goods you have brought to the parsonage.

A CALLER TOLD ME last week, "I have heard of the work that your Church has been doing!"

"IT IS GOD'S WORK we are doing, not our work," I answered. And I could have gone on, "IT IS GOD'S WORK WE WILL ALWAYS DO HERE!"

AMEN.

THE FAITHFUL SERVANT IS REWARDED

Internal Satisfaction
    External Certainty
    Eternal Salvation

November 24, 1963
    Trinity Lutheran Church, Galion, Ohio
    On the occasion of Adult Baptism and Confirmation
    The Sunday following the assassination of President
Kennedy
    Trinity XXIV

TEXT: Luke 12:42-48
    DO YOU REMEMBER the vow you took when you became a member of the Christian Church? As a catechumen, you stood before almighty God and vowed faithfulness even under the fear of death. You as a member of the Christian Church promised to live in this faith, to be diligent in the use of the means of grace, and to serve the Lord Jesus Christ to the end.
    MOST OF US have been church members now for many years—possibly in some cases more years than we care to

remember accurately. Today, a group of adults will become active participants in this congregation also be pledging faithfulness.

A TRAGEDY like that which has struck our nation with the death of our president awakens our faith for a little while. But even this kind of tragic stimulant is only temporary. For the most part, we have become tranquilized—caught up in the same monotonous pattern of life going on, death coming nearer, not much getting done.

IN THIS TRAGIC HOUR, each one of us should take the time to reevaluate ourselves in the light of our promise to God.

HERE IS A STORY told by Jesus in the twelfth chapter of Luke, beginning at the forty-second verse.

AND THE LORD said, "Who then is the faithful and wise steward, whom his master will set over his household, to give them their portion of food at the proper time? Blessed is that servant whom his master when he comes will find so doing. Truly I tell you, he will set him over all his possessions. But if that servant says to himself, 'My master is delayed in coming,' and begins to beat the manservants and the maidservants, and to eat and drink and get drunk, the master of that servant will come on a day when he does not expect him and at an hour he does not know, and will punish him, and put him with the unfaithful. And that servant who knew his master's will, but did not make ready or act according to his will, shall receive a severe beating. But he who did not know, and did what deserved a beating shall receive a light beating. Everyone to whom much is given, of him will much be required; and of him to whom men commit much, they will demand the more.

THE PARABLE TEACHES US that the faithful servant is rewarded with Internal Satisfaction, External Certainty, and Eternal Salvation.

INTERNAL SATISFACTION is one of the almost indescribable joys of being a faithful Christian. Only faithful Christians can enjoy the fruits of the spirit. Love permeates our being. Joy bubbles throughout our bloodstream. Peaceful tranquility rules our life. There is a virility of inner life much like the brilliant crackling of a log fire—the fire of the spirit of Jesus Christ. This satisfaction is our reward when we permit God to be in control of us, to be part of us, to live in us.

THIS SATISFACTION comes from faithfully doing our job in God's Kingdom. Much like the steward in our text. He was the middleman, so to speak, between the owner of the estate and the man that worked the fields. His job as holder of the stock-room keys was to give out the daily supplies to keep the estate running smoothly, as ordered by the absent master. His responsibility was to keep the place functioning on an even keel, for though the master was absent, his spirit and witness remained to guide the steward.

AS FAITHFUL SERVANTS, our task is to dole out the fruits of the spirit to all the souls around us, so the church and the kingdom of Jesus Christ may flourish.

BUT OFTEN, the faithful road to eternal life seems long and rough. It is pock-marked with ragged ruts and deep depressions. We try to follow the Christian way of life, but there are many obstacles forcing us backwards. Satan's super-salesmen are still selling us happiness wrapped up in neat packages. But after a while, not even a "combination of ingredients" will satiate the pounding mental and physical pain that our fast living has created.

LIFE IS MUCH LIKE walking in an early morning fog. We feel alone and solitary because our vision is blurred. Like the steward in the parable, we get the feeling that the task is futile. THE LORD IS NOT COMING TODAY. I'LL TRY TO BE READY TOMORROW.

BUT TIME IS RUNNING OUT! Death is just a rifle shot

away. Death is the next flat tire on a high-speed highway. Death could strike you down on the way home from church this morning.

INEVITABLY WE CAST OFF our restraint and let the lowness of our inner nature command us once more. Instead of being God-Seekers, we become Self-Seekers outside the church door WHEN WE THINK WE ARE SAFE.

MOST OF US ARE MORE SUBTLE than the man in this parable, who took advantage of his position and played the tyrant, reveling in his own lust and manipulating those around him. Our subtle hypocrisy makes WHITE just a little more dirty. And the sharply contrasting BLACK becomes sluggishly a watered-down grey.

THE UNFAITHFUL STEWARD took advantage of his temporary authority, and so have we. The Lord Jesus Christ has set up in each one of us a trust fund, and the one who squanders it will be condemned. We are faced with a heaven or hell proposition. It is about time that we do something about it. In the words of the parable, "Blessed is the man found doing the Lord's work." Yet one sure way of ending up in hell is to know the Lord's will and to do nothing about it. If the steward of our text had remained faithful, he would have received a promotion to the position of estate manager. Our reward is internal satisfaction, bringing joy, peace, patience, goodness, and gentleness.

THE FAITHFUL CHRISTIAN ALSO receives an external reward—of an EXTERNAL CERTAINTY. Our lives should be built on the same foundation as the church for which we witness—that of Jesus Christ. When others view us, they should not be able to divorce what they see from the very light of God bursting forth from the root of our being. Only God could give a man such a certainty that he becomes a mighty spiritual fortress that even the most tantalizing jibe and hateful thrust of the devil cannot run him through.

EVERY FAITHFUL MAN OF GOD has God's spirit working in him. For the greatest reward given the servant of Jesus Christ is that of the knowledge of eternal salvation. ETERNAL SALVATION. It is a reward. It is free. All we have to do is accept it.

BECAUSE EVERYTHING is given to us, much will be required of us. No one is excused, for even the heathens have the works of the law written in their hearts. Some have been given more in proportion to others. These must work to be even greater stewards. The more light that is beamed on us, the greater will be the punishable-ness of our sins. Jesus is a righteous and impartial Lord. He provides eternal salvation. He asks us in this parable to be ready on call to do his will.

AT CONFIRMATION, WE VOWED to serve Jesus Christ. Let us reaffirm that vow with these young people today and become living examples of the Lord Jesus Christ in our torn and fragile world.

AMEN.

THANK GOD FOR AMERICA

November 26, 1963
   Trinity Lutheran Church, Galion, Ohio
   Thanksgiving Message

TEXT: Psalm 92:1
   IT IS GOOD to give thanks to the Lord, to sing praises to
Thy name, O Most High, to declare Thy steadfast love in the
morning, and Thy faithfulness by night.
   IT WAS A COLD AND BLEAK November morning. The
year was 1945. A long train poked its way through the ice-covered
valleys of central Germany. A light snow had fallen. The rising
sun cast orange and blue shadows across the barren wilderness.
There was not a sign of life anywhere, except in the train which
was filled to capacity with homeless refugees fleeing the Russian
Army, moving west to freedom and a new life.
   SUDDENLY, the train lurched and twisted to a halt. "Everybody out!" someone cried. "Run for cover! Hide in the woods!
Get out of sight!" They hid in ditches, behind fallen logs, under
the protection of tall pines. There was a hushed silence.
   OUT OF THE SKY came the hum of an airplane's motor,

penetrating the hushed silence. The Russian fighter that had been harassing the refugee train since the daylight passed over the train, turned, and began its long strafing run. The sound of the machine guns drowned out the song of the early morning birds.

AS THE PLANE passed over the train, the piercing sound of a child crying sounded above all of the motors and guns. Out of one of the box cars staggered a woman, haggard and worn, holding the screaming baby to her breast.

"DON'T STAND THERE! Get down! He's coming back!" someone cried.

MACHINE GUNS again drowned out the baby's scream. The plane passed over, turned, and was gone. There was silence in the woods. The woman standing beside the train was all alone. She was weeping silently. Tightly to her breast, she held the torn and bleeding body of her infant son. Holding her baby up to the sunlight, pointing its bleeding face that was no longer a face toward heaven, she cried out, "My God, my God, why hast thou forsaken me?"

MY FRIEND Hans Goebell was on that train and he knows what is feels like to be forsaken. To be utterly cut off. Abandoned. He was there that day, riding to freedom one instant, and the next, found himself pushing his face into the frozen earth until his nose began to bleed, trying to find protection from the screaming confusion that was happening all around him.

"I NEVER THOUGHT I would be able to thank God for anything again," Hans Goebell once said to me. "I never thought I could thank God until the crowded boat I was on slowly steamed into New York harbor—and I saw the Statue of Liberty standing there in all her majesty—holding the lamp of freedom for all to see."

"I WALKED the streets of the crowded city. I saw crowds pushing. People going where they wanted to go. Children were laughing, not crying. There were bright lights everywhere. Cash drawers were ringing in the night. Church bells tolled out the glad news—GOD IS GOD AND WE ARE FREE!"

HANS GOEBELL wandered into a church that night. The bell was tolling the evening prayer. The lights were on. The doors were open. But the building was empty. Slipping into an obscure seat at the rear of the sanctuary, he knelt down and breathed the prayer of his heart: Thank you, God, for America!"

THANK YOU, GOD, FOR AMERICA! Tomorrow, we are going to gather around the dinner table for the feast of the year. We are going to thank God for many things—for the turkey and the cranberry sauce, for the day off from work, for the nice weather, for the football game on television, for the aspirin tablets that manage to get us through the day. But how many of us are going to take the time to thank God for America?

FOR YOU SEE, we Americans do not know what it is like to be forsaken, to be cut off from God. And we run the risk of taking his goodness for granted. Forty-five minutes without electricity is enough to create mass hysteria in this city. I wonder if anyone would notice if God would wander away and leave us tonight? No matter what we have done, in spite of all the empty churches, God has never forsaken this great nation of ours, or His people. He has heaped on us all of the joys of the Spirit. He has heaped on us material goods too! Not one of us will be cold tonight. Not one of us will be harassed by a fighter plane on our way home. Not one of us will go hungry tomorrow.

AND YET, God is crying out this very night to his people everywhere: "My people, my people, why have you forsaken me?"

I SUPPOSE you noticed the cartoon PEANUTS which appeared in the Sunday newspaper of a few months ago. It showed Charlie Brown sitting on the floor, watching his television set, when Lucy walks in.

"GUESS WHAT!" Lucy asked Charlie Brown.

"What?" he replies.

Lucy gets a guilty look on her face and beckons for him to follow her. They peek into the next room to see if anyone is watching or listening. They pull down all of the shades over the windows. They crawl behind the living room couch, and Lucy whispers to a shocked Charlie Brown, "WE PRAYED IN SCHOOL TODAY!"

WE HAVE TAKEN God for granted, and God is being taken away from us. America has lately been acting in the name of "Fair Play" and has forgotten to act in the name of "God." Bible reading has been taken from the schools. The pilgrims came to America because their prayers offended. Now their children cannot pray in public schools because prayers once again are an offense. It has been ruled in New York that the third stanza of "America" cannot be sung in public schools because it mentions God:

Our Father's God to thee

Author of liberty

Of Thee we sing!!!

There is a case before a California court to remove the words that the Congress of the United States placed in the Pledge of Allegiance—that we are "one nation, UNDER GOD!"

GOD HAS NOT FORSAKEN US, even though we, the Christian majority, have permitted this to happen in this great land of ours. He has forgiven those who do not have the time to come to church. He has forgiven those who do come, but only to gather into small groups and grumble and complain. But we must take great care here, lest one day soon our children will be forced to pull down all of the shades and climb behind the couch and whisper to each other: WE PRAYED IN CHURCH TODAY!!

THANK GOD FOR AMERICA!

AMEN.

MISSING THE MARK

December 1, 1963
    First Sunday in Advent, Holy Communion
    Trinity Lutheran Church, Galion, Ohio

TEXT: Isaiah 1: 18-20
    COME NOW let us reason together,
    says the Lord:
    though your sins are like scarlet,
    they shall be white as snow;
    though they are red like crimson
    they shall become like wool.
    If you are willing and obedient,
    you shall eat the good of the land;
    but if you refuse and rebel,
    you shall be devoured by the sword;
    for the mouth of the Lord has spoken.
    TWO SUNDAYS ago, I had the opportunity to visit with a
family in the rustic outdoors. After the robust noon meal had
begun to wear off, my friend and I went outside to shoot with
the bow and arrow.

NOW I AM NO MASTER, to be sure, but I used to teach archery to the Boy Scouts at summer camp. I have shot thousands of arrows. I know how to hold the bow so it is in perfect balance. I know how to properly place my feet so they are parallel to the target.

I SHOWED my companion the proper way to "nock" the arrow and how to place the fingers on the bow string. Then I drew the bow with determination, aimed, and sent the arrow swiftly and surely on its mission with a satisfying "thwatt!"

AND that arrow flew toward the target and then kept on flying over the hill and down into the next valley, missing the bullseye by a country mile.

I SHOT quite a few arrows that afternoon. They sent clods of dirt flying to the right and to the left and above the target. They were all close, but they all missed the mark. I know most of the rules about properly shooting arrows. I know enough of the established techniques of archery to get by, but the points of my arrows missed the mark.

OUR CHRISTIAN LIVES are like that—often, they miss the mark. We have all been instructed at one time or another in the rules of the Christian faith. We know only too well the mechanics of the Christian life, all the essentials necessary to master to set us on our journey toward heaven. In fact, we often know so much about so many things that we spend too much time arguing and bickering over the little points of our faith and we fail to get the one big point—that we are here to serve Christ, and if we do not serve Him, our lives miss the mark.

OUR LIVES HAVE BECOME confused and befuddled in this modern world—a world where fear seems to be holding us in its grasp. While it is true that we are afraid because the times are dangerous, it is also true that times are dangerous because we are afraid. As Robert Frost put it, "There is nothing I'm afraid of like scared people."

AS A RESULT OF OUR FEAR, we are suffering from "spiritual amnesia." A spiritual blackout, spiritual forgetfulness. We remember to do those things that on the surface look good, but we refrain from doing anything which will cause us to accept responsibility. We remember to do a little, but we forget to do much. In St. Paul's day, special notice was taken only of those few churches that were doing nothing. Today, special notice is taken of that church that does anything. That's how much we "miss the mark" 2,000 years later.

WE DO NOT ADVERTISE our personal failures. We tell the newspapers when we win a game, not when we lose. We tell the neighbors when our children make a good mark, not when they miss the mark. Yet we persist in advertising the failure of the Christian church for the whole world to see.

WE CALL OURSELVES CHRISTIANS, but we do not serve Christ. We know the *how* of religion, but we ignore the *do* of religion. We call ourselves disciples—but we know not discipline! How often we have heard remarks like these:

"SUNDAY is my only day off! When else can I sleep in and take life easy?"

"WHY, I CAN'T DO THAT! A long time ago something nasty was said, and it is still sticking in my craw. I'll never serve in that Church!"

WHAT about all those people who have retired from active Christian service? MISS THE MARK!

I SUPPOSE you have all heard about Klopp's Flop. Here is the way *Newsweek* reported the incident:

A TWIN-ENGINED CARIBOU PLANE was just about to land, when it was forcibly impressed upon General Paul Harkins, Commander of the United States forces in South Vietnam, that something was seriously wrong.

BELLS jangled and light flashed on and off. The general shouted to the crew, but no one seemed to hear him. Then he braced himself as the plane crash-landed on its belly on a dirt strip 110 miles from Saigon. Emerging from the rear door, the badly shaken general tried to control his temper, but he could not quite do it.

"THAT'S A DEVIL of a way to come down!" he roared. "Don't you know how to land a plane?"

THE PILOT, Captain Charles A. Klopp, sheepishly explained, "Well, sir, I forgot to put the wheels down." And that's how Klopp flopped!

NO MATTER how healthy a start we get in our Christian lives, if we know what to do and if we fail to do it, we will flop, like Klopp.

SIR JOHN STAINER has his chorus sing soberly at the end of "The Crucifixion"—"Is it nothing to you who pass by?" If the cross of Jesus Christ means nothing to us—if the cross of Jesus Christ does not compel us to forget ourselves and to serve Him —then in the agony and bleeding misery of his death, Jesus Christ has missed the mark. Then throughout the centuries, all of Christianity has missed the mark.

TODAY IS ADVENT SUNDAY. Today, we begin another church year. The Lord beckons us to his table. He promises us that "though our sins be scarlet, they shall be as white as snow... If we are willing and obedient, we shall eat of the good of the earth."

LET US THIS YEAR aim to serve Christ—and make his mark known to the whole world.

AMEN.

THE SAVIOR COMES IN JUDGMENT

December 8, 1963
Advent II
Trinity Lutheran Church, Galion, Ohio

TEXT: Luke 21: 25-31

PORTENTS WILL APPEAR in sun, moon, and stars. On earth, nations will stand helpless, not knowing which way to turn from the roar and surge of the sea; men will faint with terror at the thought of all that is coming upon the world; for the celestial powers will be shaken. And then they will see the Son of Man coming on a cloud with great power and glory. When all this begins to happen, stand upright and hold your heads high, because your liberation is near.

HE TOLD THEM THIS PARABLE: "Look at the fig tree, or my other tree. As soon as it buds, you can see for yourselves that summer is near. In the same way, when you see all this happening, you may be sure that the kingdom of God is near.

MOST OF US look at ourselves in a mirror every day that we live, whether it be to shave, to comb our hair, or for the sheer enjoyment of it. Most of us are not disappointed in the image we see reflected from the mirror.

YET when we look at our image in the mirror of God's Word, what a strange monster we see—distorted and disjointed. It is our nature as sinful people to have our head where our heart ought to be. Our heart is set on the things of this earth. Earth is for walking on. We should be treading the things of this world under our feet.

IN THE MIRROR OF GOD'S WORD, our big toe is where our heart should be. All too often we find ourselves kicking against the God of heaven when we ought to be setting our hearts on things above.

AS THE SUN BEGINS TO SHINE and the earth awakens— excitement of the holiday season, more than at any time of the year—we see evidenced all around us that the earth has become our heaven. We see suns in its muddy pools and stars in all of its filth.

THE SAVIOR is coming again in judgment, our text tells us today. God is coming with a tremendous cosmic force. All of the signs of the Lord's coming are here today. Jesus told his disciples that the powers of heaven would become dislocated. How tremendous forces will spin planets out of orbit and into orbit. Light will disappear. The world will sink into deep darkness. No day will dawn. We will look to the sky and to the sea for light and hope...and we will find only terror, torture, tempest, and trial.

SUCH A HOLOCAUST is completely beyond human conception. But here we see it spoken by the child of God—by the child of God who will bring it to pass.

THE SIGNS ARE SHOUTING the coming of God's judgment. And while they shout, we stand and stare and stall. We are standing at the crossroad of life and death, and here we are forced to make a choice—to go one way or another. Even a simple choice like this involves a renunciation. If we choose to follow one road, we must forego the delights of the other.

OFTEN WE ARE NOT willing to do this. We do not wish to commit ourselves completely. We would like to keep the options open. After all, why not play it safe?

WE WOULD LIKE TO walk one road toward our goal and at the same time enjoy detouring into the delights of the other road as well. The late beloved poet Robert Frost put this dilemma of life into a few lines which he called, "The Road Not Taken." He says:

Two roads diverged in a yellow wood,
   And sorry I could not travel both
   And be one traveler, long I stood
   And looked down one as far as I could
   To where it bent in the underground;
   Then I took the other.

Oh, I kept the first for another day!
   Yet knowing how way leads on to way,
   I doubted if I should ever come back.
   I shall be telling you this with a sign
   Somewhere ages and ages hence:
   Two roads diverged in a wood, and I—
   I took the one less traveled by,
   And that has made all the difference.

THE JUDGMENT IS COMING. We are at the crossroad of life or death. Some of us glance to the right and to the left down both roads and then choose by whim and go about our merry way as carefree as Br'er Rabbit, zip-a-dee-doo-dah-ing through life—playing with eternal death.

TOO MANY OF US stand at the fork of the road, fingering

our whiskers and scratching our head, unable to decide, letting all the pros balance out the cons. And suddenly we find ourselves off the track and bogged down, with little or no chance for progress. There we stand—just innocent bystanders on the road of life.

IRVING S. COBB once said, "In politics I'm a Democrat; in religion I'm an innocent bystander." But there are no innocent bystanders in Christianity! Christ told his followers: "The one who is not for is me against me!" If we do not commit ourselves to Christ and walk God's way, then we are automatically against God.

FACING CHRIST is like facing the fork of the road. We come face to face with decision or indecision. In between are only ragged ruts and deep depression. We have to decide and then face the responsibility of that decision.

WHEN SAINT AUGUSTINE was young, he found the world attractive. Anyone who has read his Confessions knows how patiently his Christian mother taught him of the severe judgment of Christ and of how she did her best to lead him along the right road of life.

YET young Augustine found the signs and wonders of the world enticing. Sin was a stronger temptation than he cared to resist. Finally, to quiet the compelling force of conscience, he prayed, "Make me pure, O Lord, but not yet!"

THIS HAS BEEN THE CRY of uncommitted Christians everywhere. "Judge me righteously, O Lord—tomorrow!" Tomorrow—when I have had time to shine my shoes and fix my hair. Tomorrow—on Monday, they are usually blue anyway. Tomorrow—after the party is over, I'll be willing to go home.

WE EARNESTLY sing on Sunday mornings, "Take my life and let it be—consecrated Lord to Thee!" But how indignant we would be if the Lord took us up on the bargain and said, "Okay, I'll take your life!"

YES, LORD, TAKE MY LIFE—after I have lived three score years and ten, after I have done all of the things I want to do and after I have seen all of the things I want to see. After *I'm* done with this life—take it, Lord, and consecrate it to your service.

FROM THE CIVIL WAR comes the story of eighteen-year-old Willie Lear of Palmyra, Missouri. In 1852, the Union army occupied and had control of this area. Outrages were being committed on both sides. Union soldiers were being shot from ambush and their bodies foully mutilated.

TO AVENGE and stamp out these atrocities, the federal commander arrested and imprisoned a large number of the citizens of Palmyra, charging them with being guerillas. By court-martial, all were judged and sentenced to be shot, including Willie Lear.

THE COMMANDER DECIDED to select ten men for immediate execution, and reserve the remainder for future punishment if the outrages continued. These ten were drawn by lot. Willie Lear was not among them.

BUT A POOR neighbor with a large family was selected for immediate execution. His death would leave his family in a helpless condition.

WILLIE NOTED his neighbor's agony and was deeply moved. He stepped up to his commanding officer and offered to take his neighbor's place.

THE OFFICER had no objection as the order read only that ten men were to be shot. As long as that number was made up, the law was satisfied. The neighbor accepted Lear as his substitute and the whole matter was settled.

WILLIE LEAR fell before the firing squad. As the man for whom he died looked at the bloody and torn flesh of Willie Lear's mangled body, his tears fell and lay in the palm of the dead man's outstretched hand. All he could say was, "He died for me! He died for me! I am free!"

MIRRORED in the Word of God, we stand condemned. Our days are ending. We have been judged and found guilty. Only a death will satisfy the law. Eternal death is the just punishment for our sins. But on the cross—Jesus Christ our Judge has satisfied the law. He has taken our place. He has died for us. We are free! Free! If we take the straight road—if we take hold of God's outstretched hand and follow God down the path of eternal life. GOD DIED FOR YOU! YOU ARE FREE! YOU ARE FREE!!

AMEN.

HOME FOR CHRISTMAS

December 22, 1963
  Trinity Lutheran Church, Galion, Ohio
  Advent IV
  The Sunday Morning before Christmas

CHRISTMAS IS THE TIME OF YEAR for telling stories. The family gathers together under the newly decorated tree. If you are lucky and have a fireplace, the fire shadows dance across the room as the last log burns brightly. and then dies away to flowing embers, filling the room with sweet cherry smoke.

THAT IS HOW we used to gather at our house on Christmas Eve. In our pajamas, heavy slippers on our feet, anxious anticipation in our hearts. Dad would take our family Bible—sit with us under the Christmas tree and tell us our annual Christmas story.

NO MATTER how we look at it, this is a perilous world in which we live. Everything is not going right and sometimes the things that sinful men and women do drive us to distraction—or at least to the medicine cabinet.

THERE ARE MANY THINGS I could say to you this morning, but somehow they are out of place this time of the year. This is not a time for chiding—but for caroling and charity. Not for goading—but for good will and peace among men.

RATHER than preach this morning, I am going to tell you a story. For more truly than anything else, you are my family this year.

I AM GOING TO BEGIN like my father always did, by reading the Christmas story from the second chapter of St. Luke.

IN THOSE DAYS a decree went out from Caesar Augustus that all the world should be enrolled. This was the first enrollment, when Quirinius was governor of Syria. And all went to be enrolled, each to his own city. And Joseph also went up from Galilee, from the city of Nazareth, to Judea, to the city of David, which is called Bethlehem, because he was of the house and lineage of David, to be enrolled with Mary, his betrothed, who was with child. And while they were there, the time came for her to be delivered. And she gave birth to her firstborn son, wrapped him in swaddling clothes, and laid him in a manger, because there was no place for them in the inn.

AND IN THAT REGION, there were shepherds out in the field, keeping watch over their flock by night. And an angel of the Lord appeared to them, and the glory of the Lord shone around them, and they were filled with fear. And the angel said to them, "Be not afraid; for behold, I bring you good news of great joy which will come to all the people; for to you is born this day in the city of David a Savior, who is Christ the Lord. And this will be a sign for you: you will find a babe wrapped in swaddling clothes and lying in a manger." And suddenly, there was with the angel a multitude of the heavenly host praising God and saying,"

"Glory to God in the highest,
and on earth peace among men with whom
he is pleased!

WHEN THE ANGELS went away from them into heaven, the shepherds said to one another, "Let us go over to Bethlehem and see this thing that has happened, which the Lord has made known to us." And they went with haste, and found Mary and Joseph, and the babe lying in a manger. And when they saw it, they made known the saying which had been told them concerning this child; and all who heard it wondered at what the shepherds told them. But Mary kept all these things, pondering them in her heart.

IT WAS A BITTER COLD Christmas Eve in 1960. The big old church in Baltimore was filled with people for the Christmas service. I had finished reading the Christmas story. The choir had sung. Mary Adams had spilled her music all over the floor. A baby was crying in the back row. The good doctor was droning away in the pulpit. The people looked as if they were listening, but I wasn't. I did not have time for church that Christmas Eve.

I WAS WORRIED about catching the 12:20 train, and time was running out.

"HOME FOR CHRISTMAS!" I thought. A warm glow spread through me. "You are foolish to go," they all said. "You will only have five hours at home if you are going to be back for Sunday communion."

AT LAST the service ended. I tossed off my robes and pulled on my overcoat. Before I stepped out into the snow, I carefully wrapped a scarf around my clerical collar, so no one would know who I was.

"VICAR BILL! Merry Christmas, Vicar Bill!" came a youthful voice I recognized.

BUCKY, the newsboy, stood on the corner. He still had an armload of the final edition. He would stand there until they were all gone.

I picked up a paper and gave him a bill. "Keep the change.

Merry Christmas!" I called as the taxi rushed me to Camden Station.

"THERE'S nothing merry about Christmas!" the cabby groaned, and then fell silent with a scowl on his face.

"The Christ Child came," I mumbled to myself as the taxi knifed through the snowflakes.

THE TICKET SELLER was counting nickels when I arrived. "You'll have to run to get the 12:20. She's arriving at Gate 3."

"MERRY CHRISTMAS!" I said.

There was no answer. He was counting nickels again.

THE B&O #45 was well on its way to Washington, D.C. by the time I had stowed my bag and taken a seat by a frosted window in the center of the old car. The car was empty. I was alone. Not many people travel on Christmas Eve. Somewhere, men were singing—the pastors probably:

"Silent night. Holy night.

All is calm—"

ALL WAS NOT CALM at Martinsburg. The train hurried to a halt—hissing steam and squealing breaks. A gray old man got in. His overalls were dirty and torn. He smelled of grease and grime. He carried a shopping bag. It was filled with bottles, I thought, for I could hear glass grinding against glass.

"TRAVELING, TOM?" the conductor inquired as he passed through.

"Always go home for Christmas," came the thick, hard reply.

THE TRAIN shuttered on. The silence was broken only by glass grinding against glass. Old Tom began to sing:

"Round yon Virgin—

Mudder an' child—"

The bottles clanked again.

I LOOKED UP. Tom was standing over me. His free arm was draped around my clerical collar. He was smiling. His nose was aglow like a Christmas tree.

"How 'bout a drink, Fadder? It's Christmas Eve!"

I said no, politely thanked him, and wished him a merry Christmas. Old Tom went back to his seat.

IT WAS AT HARPER'S FERRY that they got on. The woman and the two small children. She was carrying a decorated Christmas tree. The little boy was no older than five years. In one hand, he carried a cardboard nativity. He pulled his younger sister up the aisle with the other. She was carrying a panda bear.

THE LITTLE GIRL cradled the panda bear in her arms and said softly, "Now you behave on the train if you want to go home for Christmas!"

I LOOKED OVER AT HER and winked.

She smiled. Her eager eyes told me she knew that I knew what it was like to talk to Panda Bears. "We are going home for Christmas," the little girl confided to me.

HER BROTHER TOOK UP THE CAROL: "Sleep in heavenly peace—"

The baby had fallen out of the manger in his nativity. Carefully, he placed the babe back on the hay as he sang, "Sleep in heavenly peace..."

His sister already was asleep. His head dropped to her shoulder and he joined her in the land of sugar plums.

IT WAS THEN I noticed that the mother was weeping. She was not making a sound, but tears streaked her cheeks as she sat beside the Christmas tree.

"I AM SORRY you are sad," I began.

"I'M NOT SAD. It's Christmas and I'm going to see my husband," she replied. "I have not seen him for three years. Do you know what it is like to not talk to someone you love for three years? I found out this morning I've got cancer and I'm going to die. All of a sudden, nothing mattered but Christmas and going home. So I picked up the tree and the kids. WE'RE GOING HOME for Christmas."

THE TRAIN slowed down and stopped somewhere in the Cumberland Valley. There were lights everywhere. I had heard that there had been a train wreck, so I moved out onto the platform between the cars where I could see.

WRECKAGE WAS everywhere. Boxcars on their sides; boxcars split open. It was a serene, silent night, hushed by the softness of the snow. A solitary light on top of a crane hung over the scene like a Christmas star. There was color everywhere. A cargo of plastic buckets and dishpans were strewn over the hill and into the valley, dotting the snow with red, green, and yellow.

I ALWAYS HAVE THOUGHT that if the Christ child were to be born today, he would find refuge in an empty box car. There is not any place on earth more desolate and cold than an empty boxcar in the winter. His mother would probably cradle the babe in a plastic dishpan instead of a manger, on shredded newspaper instead of hay.

A RED DISHPAN lay beside the track. It was partly filled with snow. *The Christ child will need a blanket if he comes tonight*, I said to myself. I threw down the newspaper that I had carried from Baltimore. I fell face-up over the dishpan. The train whistle shrilled in the cold night air. The words of the headline seared my consciousness like a hot iron.

543 TO DIE ON ROADS THIS CHRISTMAS. A fitting blanket for the Christ child. The train shuttered and moved on.

IT WAS DAYLIGHT when I placed my key in the lock of the front door and turned it quietly. The bells of the Presbyterian church were chiming out the news of Christmas morning. My old dog padded over and treated me as if I had been expected. Together, we picked our way through all of the torn Christmas wrappings and boxes to the kitchen.

MOTHER was sitting alone, drinking a cup of coffee.

"MERRY CHRISTMAS!" I said.

STARTLED, she turned. Tears welled in her eyes. All she could say was: "You've come home!"

"I told you we would always be together at Christmas."

The church bells crisply caroled across the Christmas morning.

"Joy to the World—The Lord had Come!"

HOME FOR CHRISTMAS!

AMEN.

X-RAYING THE SOUL

December 29, 1963
Trinity Lutheran Church, Galion, Ohio
The First Sunday After Christmas

TEXT: GALATIANS 4: 1-7

I MEAN THAT THE HEIR, as long as he is a child, is no better than a slave, though he is the owner of all the estate; but he is under the guardians and trustees until the date set by the father. So with us; when we were children, we were slaves to the elemental spirits of the universe. But when the time had fully come, God sent forth his Son, born of woman, born under the law, to redeem those who were under the law, so that we might receive adoption as sons. And because you are sons, God has sent the Spirit of his Son into our hearts, crying, "Abba! Father!" So through God, you are no longer a slave but a son, and if a son then an heir.

THE HEAD RADIOLOGIST in a large medical institution complained of persistent indigestion. One of his staff members urged he have a series of X-rays made. This he did. In this particular institution, X-ray films were designated by number only as they were sent through the department.

THE DAY following the making of the X-rays, a large number of films were placed on the radiologist's desk. When he came to the ones taken of himself, not knowing they were his, he wrote, "Inoperable cancer of the stomach." And it was.

IF THERE WERE SUCH A THING AS a spiritual X-ray that could take pictures of the true condition of the soul, and we could see a picture of our own condition, we would probably without any hesitation write, "INOPERABLE!" "NO HOPE LEFT!" And without a doubt, we would be correct from the standpoint of human skill. We have all sinned—and we are going to die!

SAINT PAUL SAYS, "For all have sinned and come short of the glory of God." This is the diagnosis of the great apostle of the Gentiles. It may seem a terrible thing to indict the whole human race with sin. It may not be credible, but it is true, whether we believe it or not.

LOOK AT THIS MORNING'S NEWSPAPER and you will see that the whole world is in bondage to sin. There is war in Viet Nam. There is rumor of a war in Cyprus. There are accusations, murders, adultery, incest. Little Orphan Annie is in trouble again, and Alley Oop is lost in a swamp.

WHEN WE LOOK at our own lives, we see that we are in bondage to sin. Saint Paul in our text says that we are slaves to the elemental spirits of the universe. Have you ever noticed how noisy our world has become? We have telephones that ring and tea-kettles that sing. We have a radio in the kitchen, a television set in the living room, and a stereo in the den. The water taps clank. The automobile washer thumps. My dog snores. We have become so accustomed to noise and confusion, uncertainty and unrest, that it is silence that becomes unbearable. They used to say no news is good news. Today, no news means there is trouble!

ALL OF LIFE suddenly seems awful. Weighed down with the externals of this world, modern man finds himself backed up against a wall, crying out, "Why was I born?"

THE INTELLECTUAL world has provided many answers to the question, "Why Was I Born?"

To be happy, says the Greek philosopher.

To help others, says the humanitarian.

To find ourselves, says the pagan psychologist.

BUT these are only half-answers. Jesus says the total reason for our existence is to be united with the Father and to live with God for eternity. Happiness alone is too uncertain a reward, too meager a goal for this life. The seeker of worldly happiness lives in unreality, in a soap-opera dream world of slobbering sentimentality.

THE READER'S DIGEST once carried this note: "In a small-town survey of domestic relations, husbands and wives were sent questionnaires to fill in. In the space for noting causes of friction in the home, one man wrote, "Me!"

IT IS QUITE POSSIBLE that if many of us were to fill in such a questionnaire, we could write what this honest man wrote.

I AM LIKE YOU ARE. I find it difficult to live the Christian life, even at Christmastime. Facing the unreality of today and the uncertainty of the future, I find it difficult to say just exactly what the Christian life should be. When it comes to Christian living, most of the world's Christians do not agree on how it should or should not be done.

I WAS FIXING an electric motor once. I had the parts spread out over the table and I thought things were going fine. A friend of mine had come in and was watching my progress with great concern. Finally, he said, "I don't know anything about electric motors, but the way you are doing that is all wrong!"

NO DOUBT you get a lot of advice about how to raise your children, what detergent to use, and how to fix hamburger so that it tastes like steak. We cannot even agree about children, detergents, or hamburger. How can we expect to agree on how Christians ought to act?

BEFORE I WAS ORDAINED, I had definite ideas about how a minister ought to act. In fact, that is exactly what I expected my pastor to do—to act. To perform as if we were puppets and he were holding the strings. I could not accept him as a fellow human being in conflict with sin.

I AM JUST LIKE YOU ARE—flesh and blood. It is nerves that make me shake. It is tension that makes me shout and explode. I have a difficult time with sin and guilt. I get discouraged. I am certain of the victory of Christ, but how often we trade certainty for complacency. When things begin to get tough, we murmur and complain.

HERE IS A STORY:

WAY BACK in the hills of upstate New York, where a lot of poor tenant farmers live, there was a wise old man whom everybody came to with their troubles. One day, a woman came to him with a sad story. She and her husband and four children lived in a one-room cabin and she said it was simply unbearable. The old man asked her if she had any chickens on the farm. When she said she did, he advised her to put the chickens in her house.

THE NEXT DAY when she came back, she said that things were even worse—much worse. Then the old man asked if she owned any cows, and when she said she had two of them, he said: "Put those two cows in the house." She did, and the next day she came back and said the place was getting to be a horror.

SO THE OLD MAN said to her, "You got a horse?" She said

that she did. "Put the horse into your house." The woman did that, too, and the following day said it was just too much—it was awful. Then the old man said to her, "Well, my dear, now take the horse and those cows and those chickens and get them all out of there, and then come back and tell me how things are."

AND THE NEXT DAY, the woman came back and said, "Thank you, oh, thank you so much. You can't imagine how comfortable we all are at last!"

BLESSINGS sometimes come in heavy disguises.

OUT OF HIS GREAT WISDOM and understanding, God knows we are discouraged. He knows we feel guilty. A feeling of guilt is the result of the knowledge that we are sinners, and as such the feeling is a good thing. It should be properly recognized as a right thing and dealt with in the proper way. There is such a thing as an unhealthy sense of guilt, and it can be left to fester and become a psychological problem, but this does not need to happen.

IN FACT, a man without a sense of guilt becomes a monster. The Nazis who slaughtered millions during the horrific years when they ruled Germany may not have been entirely free from guilty feelings, but they acted as though they were. Some who have been brought to trial since the war still give the impression that they do not feel guilt for what they did.

WHAT WE ARE AFRAID of today is not missiles, but men. The island of Cuba could be stacked high with atomic bombs and chemical and biological weapons, yet the United States, or any other nation, would not be in the slightest danger, if the people who controlled the island were entirely trustworthy.

IT ALL COMES BACK to the point that we are sinners. Wars are caused by people, not by weapons. Rumors of war are spread by people, not by telephone poles or typewriters.

THIS HARD KNOWLEDGE of human depravity need not lead us to despair. It did not lead Saint Paul to despair. He affectionately calls us children in our text. He was a clear-eyed realist when he assessed human nature. It is impossible to reform humanity, but it is entirely possible for God to redeem and recreate it. This is why Christ came and died—to buy us out of the slavery of sin and make us whole. He conquered sin once and for all so that we may conquer sin. In Christ, we are no longer slaves of sin, but sons of God. And if we are sons of God, we become heirs, inheritors of eternal life.

GOD HAD A NEW EARTH ONCE, in the beginning. Sin ruined it. But sin did not ruin the plan of God for a perfect world with sinless people.

NEVER has the world needed Christ so badly as it does now. Never has the church so badly needed to realize its real mission as it does today. Never have we, individually, so badly needed to accept each other as we really are and be willing to become new creatures so we may be fitted for eternal life.

BE STILL AND KNOW GOD

December 31, 1963
  Trinity Lutheran Church, Galion, Ohio
  New Year's Eve

TEXT: Psalm 46:10
  BE STILL and know that I am God.
  THERE IS A WINDING road running through the hills of Maryland, along the shores of the beautiful Potomac. A few years ago, that old road was reconstructed into a concrete highway. From the moment it opened, there were daily traffic accidents. In order to check this menace, the highway commission constructed road signs at dangerous curves proclaiming, "This road is not foolproof."
  WE COULD very well say this evening: 1964 is not foolproof. It is with excitement that we stand before the new year. All of us are glad the old year is over. For most of us, life is already a well-traveled road. We know our way. We know where we would like to go. But on January first, it is always good to start out on a new road.
  AS WE stand on the threshold of a new year—of what many

of us believe to be a new world—there is a solemn demand for caution. The psalmist in our text says, "Stop! Be still...and know that I am God." Be silent! Keep quiet.

IF THERE IS ANYTHING we moderns fear, it is silence. Yet if there is anything we need on the eve of 1964, it is silence— silence enough to let God speak to us and direct our lives.

SOREN KIERKEGAARD, the Danish Lutheran theologian, has said, "The present state of the world and the whole of life is diseased. If I were a doctor and were asked for my advice, I would reply: Create silence. Men today fear silence as they fear solitude, because both give them a glimpse of the terror of life's nothingness."

OUR DAYS ARE SHOT through with haste. The man of the hour is the man out of breath. The quick lunch, the hurried prayer, the swift flight—all these are characteristic of the lives we have led in 1963.

BUSY WITH DAILY ACTIVITIES and encompassed by sounds, we pour things into our minds and hearts, never stopping to think through this accumulation. No wonder our lives at the beginning of a near year are full of clamor, clutter, and confusion.

ON THE EVE of the new year we need a time of quiet—the healing touch of quiet, a deep immersion into inner peace, wherein we may inquire, "Is it well with my soul?"

QUEEN JULIANA of the Netherlands once said, "Everyone should try to find a spot to be alone, in order to have a proper opportunity to concentrate and to think." Jesus often sought to be alone, often reflecting on the words of Psalm 23: "He makes me to lie down in green pastures. He leads me beside still water; he restores my soul."

TRUE SILENCE with God rests in the mind and gives nourishment to the soul. Picture Washington at Valley Forge, kneeling to pray in the snow. Here the father of our country was utilizing the privilege of being alone with God. Here he found his courage to face the new day.

I MUST say to this you once again, and I must say it so clearly that no one will misunderstand. We can only build a new life when we put God back into the center of life.

TO BEGIN the new year without God, without his spiritual support, is like making a watch run with a broken mainspring. To build the new year without God is like putting gravel into mortar, which will quickly crumble.

WE OFTEN QUESTION ourselves. "What are we here for? What is life all about? What is the good of it all?"

IN 1964, these questions will only be answered by those who walk through life cautiously—who stop, look, and listen—and see God standing in the center of the universe.

AMEN.

LET US FORGET, LEST WE FORGET

January 5, 1964
   Trinity Lutheran Church, Galion, Ohio
   Second Sunday After Christmas

TEXT: I Timothy 6:11-14.
   BUT AS FOR YOU MAN OF GOD ... aim at righteousness, godliness, faith, love, steadfastness, gentleness. Fight the good fight of the faith; take hold of the eternal life to which you were called when you made the good confession in the presence of many witnesses. In the presence of God, who gives life to all things, and of Christ Jesus who in his testimony before Pontius Pilate made the good confession, I charge you to keep the commandment unstained and free from reproach until the appearing of our Lord Jesus Christ.
   "MANY A MAN fails to become a thinker for sole reason that his memory is too good."
   THIS STATEMENT WAS made by Nietzsche, a German philosopher. Today, we are living in a time when only the advantages of good memory are spoken of. The skills of psychologists and educators are dedicated to the strengthening of our memo-

ries. College curricula and courses in adult education are sched-
uled with the purpose of developing memory efficiency.

J. M. BARRIE spoke up for good memory in this vein: "God
gave us our memories so that we might have roses in
December."

OF COURSE this is true. Yet a young man of ten tender
years had a point, too, when he said, "My memory is the thing I
forget with!"

WHAT I AM TRYING TO SAY is that there are times when
we should cultivate the habit of forgetfulness. I must admit that
I never observed courses in forgetfulness in any college cata-
logue that I have read. But nevertheless, at the dawn of 1964, the
ability to forget is essential to our happiness and satisfaction in
life.

FOR INSTANCE, we should learn to forget the sharp words
spoken to us by wives, husbands, sisters, brothers, or friends.
This kind of forgetfulness will enhance our remembrance of
their kindnesses to us through the years. When the memory is
cleared of bitterness, we can better recall the wonderful times
shared together in helpful struggle.

FOR 1964, may I suggest the following:

FORGET the gossip you almost enjoyed listening to. Forget
you ever heard it, for it may not be true, and you may be
tempted to pass it on. You know how gossip can grow and
destroy. The end effect may sound a thousand times worse than
when you heard it.

FORGET the peculiarities of people you love. If all of us
were cut from one pattern, if all of us had the same tempera-
ment, think of how dull we would be!

FORGET all of the unfair treatment you received in 1963. Do
not let it make you sour on life. Do not let it fill your eyes with
the glassy gleam of revenge or your hearts with the black bile of
hate. It is a pity when we allow ourselves to dwell on a few bad

things so long that we fail to see any of the good things with which God is blessing us constantly. And when you think that you have been neglected or forgotten, forget that too! Lew Wallace was right when he had Ben Hur say, "Oh, if in being forgotten, we could only forget!"

FORGET your own wrongdoings. God has forgiven us. The grace of God makes all of this possible. We must let all of our failures of the past be lost in our sanctified ambition to serve God better in 1964—lost in our enthusiasm to be better persons today than we were yesterday.

THIS KIND OF FORGETFULNESS will count as an asset to our character and our church—not a liability. Families, nations, churches, the whole world would be much better off than they are today if they would place as much emphasis on proper forgetting as they do on efficient remembering.

AIDÉ had life straight when he mused:

"I sit beside my lonely fire
And pray for wisdom yet:
For calmness to remember
Or courage to forget.

OFTENTIMES, we get so wrapped up in our own discouragements and disappointments that we fail to make any progress. Saint Paul feels that Christians have no right to become so distracted by themselves that they remain aloof from the society to which they belong. As Christians, we must forget our petty differences and show the entire world what God has done for us here.

WE ARE LIVING IN AN AGE when the word of God is no longer popular. The Bible is no longer the outstanding bestseller. The *Saturday Review* listed Mitford's *The High Cost of Dying* as a runaway favorite over God's Book of Life. We are living in a time when preaching is no longer listened to.

I SAY, in 1964, let us make this word of God popular. Let us carry this word of God out to Galion and set people free. Let us do what they all say cannot be done. Let us save souls in a town where almost everyone belongs to a church.

LET US catch the fire of the Spirit and move with the power of God. People will take notice. They already have. Not even Galion can turn its back on a dedicated people of God fighting for their faith.

WE MUST LIVE IN THIS TOWN as a people transformed by Christ—not self-centered or self-righteous, but secure— secure in the fact that everything we have has come from God and that to serve him is our one mission in life.

AND IT CAN BEGIN WITH YOU—one person working for God. Not a crowd, just you. For nearly a century after Paul, we do not read in the Bible of any one great missionary, of any one outstanding man of God. Yet the first century was a great century of missionary progress. The whole Christian Church was carrying on a silent and unconscious campaign. By simply living the Christian life in the middle of a heathen nation, the early Christians, year after year, bore witness to the new spiritual power of Jesus Christ.

IT ONLY takes one person doing the work of Christ. Just one. Here is a legend of ancient Rome:

FOR ENTERTAINMENT in pagan Rome, the people would go the arena to watch the gladiator contests, much as we go to a football game today. Only they had to go themselves. They could not watch the Rose Bowl on television. Today at the beginning of a game, we sing the *Star-Spangled Banner* before we allow our modern gladiators to hit each other. In pagan Rome, the gladiators would parade across the arena smartly and stand stiffly before the Emperor's Box. They would raise their armor so that it shone in the sun and say, "WE who are about to die salute thee!"

THEIR VOICES were drowned by the cheers of the crowd, and they went about the business of living or dying. In a few minutes, bodies and blood would bloat the arena in a bath of death. The flies had a feast. The crowd cheered and drank wine from leather pouches.

IT IS SAID that on one such afternoon, a solitary citizen stood in the middle of the grandstand and shouted, "No! Stop! Thou shalt not kill!"

NOT MANY heard because of the wine and the noise. Few noticed him until he made his way to the center of the arena where the last two gladiators were fighting to the death. The crowd hushed. The Christian ran between the gladiators and shouted, "Stop! Thou shalt not kill!"

ONE OF THE GLADIATORS raised his sword and with one stroke ran him through. The Christian fell to the sand. The crowd cheered and drank wine. The gladiators stepped over his body, and the fight went on.

SOMEWHERE at the top of the coliseum, a man shrugged his shoulders, got up, and left. Another followed him, and another. They did not all leave that day, but eventually they did, and Rome had to stop having gladiator fights because nobody came.

JUST ONE MAN—and a whole nation changed its habits. Just one man doing the work of Christ. Just one Christ came, and the world has not been the same since.

TOMORROW, on January 6, we celebrate the festival of the Epiphany. It tells of the sudden silent coming of Christ into our lives. The coming of Christ brings a new dawn for us—not just a new year, but a new life, a new hope. The coming of Christ brings with it knowledge that not one of us could have gained for ourselves—that God is gracious, that God is good, that God cares, that God has not forgotten.

WE DARE NOT let the horrors of 1963 blind us to the hope

of 1964. We must forget ourselves, lest we forget God. We must forge ahead with Christ, lest we forfeit our eternal happiness. We dare not fight each other, the vicar, the pastor, the community, and flounder in sin. But let us fight for Christ, so his word may flower forever.

AMEN.

FACE UP TO GOD

January 12, 1964
  Trinity Lutheran Church, Galion, Ohio
  First Sunday After Epiphany

Day of the first bulletin in color

TEXT: Roman 12: 1-5.

I APPEAL to you therefore, brethren, by the mercies of God, to present your bodies as a living sacrifice, holy and acceptable to God, which is your spiritual worship. Do not be conformed to this world but be transformed by the renewal of your mind, that you may prove what is the will of God, what is good and acceptable and perfect.

FOR BY THE GRACE given to me, I bid every one among you not to think of himself more highly than he ought to think, but to think with sober judgment, each according to the measure of faith which God has assigned him. For as in one body we have many members, and all the members do not have the same function, so we, though many, are one body in Christ, and individually members one of another.

SEVERAL YEARS AGO, a leading picture magazine featured a scene without identifying it or giving any indication of its location. The full-page picture permitted the viewer to form his own conclusions about what was happening.

ALL THAT COULD BE SEEN by those who looked at the picture in the magazine was a group of apparently well-fed, well-clothed, and obviously well-to-do men and women, all of whom were staring at the same thing.

EACH FACE among those prosperous people reflected unhappiness, fear, dread, or anxiety. There was not one happy or smiling face in that entire group of a dozen or so men and women.

NOTICING the lamppost and the signs, I assumed the crowd was gathered on a city street corner. I suspected a traffic accident in which one or more persons were seriously injured was the object of their concentration. Yet their facial expressions were not of the sort usually associated with shock or pity because of the suffering of someone else.

AS I LOOKED further into the faces of these people caught by the camera in a human drama, I noticed these faces reflected fear or anxiety of a deep personal nature. I had seen that expression so often in my study, in the hospital corridor—all the places people come into contact with and conflict with living and dying.

WHAT WAS THE TRAGEDY they were facing? The answer to the problem was found on the next page of the magazine. It was as startling as it was simple.

A NEWSPAPER PHOTOGRAPHER had been on his way to an assignment. He stopped at a city street intersection to wait his turn to cross the busy street. While waiting, he looked over to the people opposite him who were also waiting to cross the street.

THE PHOTOGRAPHER was struck by the expressions on

the faces of all that he saw. He quickly photographed the scene with the faces of the people in the center of his picture.

AT WHAT WERE those people staring? They were waiting for the red traffic light to turn green so that they could cross the street. That was all! The anxiety on their faces came from within them, not from the scene before their eyes. It was the hurt of their souls reflected in their eyes!

THESE WERE AMERICANS—just like we are Americans—whose country is the richest, the most powerful, and potentially the freest that the history of the world has ever known. We who are in this sanctuary this morning are envied throughout the world for what we have.

WHAT IS WRONG WITH US? We have enough to eat. We have clothes to wear. We have money to spend and a little to spare. But our faces—the mirrors of our souls—show tragedy, trial, and terror. Have we heaped up all of the riches of the material world—television sets, automobiles, bank accounts, deep freezes—and lost our souls? Have we looked out so long to the things of this world that we have forgotten to look up to God?

I HAVE HEARD IT SAID SO OFTEN, "Oh, if I could only get a little money, everything would be all right!" "If only I had a few dollars in the bank, I would be free!" Yet I have seen people who have gotten money, and things did not turn out all right. Without a God-directed goal in life, they usually don't. Worldly riches require responsibility. The riches of the Kingdom of God require responsibility too!

I REMEMBER another picture that was once found in all of the elementary schools of an earlier day. This picture was called, "Pilgrims Going to Church."

THE ARTIST pictured these people completely different from the photograph representing our present-day American scene. The Pilgrims were pictured as a confident, victorious people on their way to church. There was not one suggestion of fear or anxiety painted on their faces. The father had the Bible under his arm and a rifle on his shoulder. They were determined to face life—believing that those who looked to God and acted in faith were guided by the Holy Spirit to victory over the world.

THE EARLY PILGRIIMS were not spiritual hobos like many would lead us to believe. They sincerely believed that looking up to God was one of the most important things in life. So they gave up their relatives, their farms, businesses, and personal possessions to come to a raw, new world that was completely lacking in the comforts of life as they had known them.

THESE WERE NOT penniless people driven by poverty to seek a new life! They were substantial literate citizens, who were willing for the sake of their God to face the dangers of a new experience in a new world. It took God-given courage to come to a world that did not have a house, a building, an industry, or a church in it!

DISEASE and suffering claimed most of their lives during the first years, but they remained and conquered the wilderness. With their hands on the plow and their eyes on God, they built houses, and they built churches. They gave up the world and saved their own souls.

YES, they were obstinate, hard-headed, and at times intolerant of those with lesser stamina or with those who disagreed with them. But they were made of the stern stuff that produces greatness. Because they looked to God for power and then used their own hands in his service, we as a people shall eternally be in their debt.

I SEE THIS SAME STERN STUFF that produces greatness in people here this morning. With your eyes on God's promise, you came here and built this beautiful church on a garbage heap some thirty years ago. Putting your hands on the ax, and your backs to the plow, and your hearts to prayer, you built this church. Out of nothing, you really made something during a depression when you had nothing, for you placed yourselves in the hands of God.

WHAT A GLORIOUS DAY it was when the day of dedication came. I have read many times the booklet you printed up for that grand occasion. Then you came up and sat down in your church, and that is exactly where we still are today—sitting. At least those of you who can find a seat are sitting!

BUT BUILDING A CHURCH DID NOT COMPLETE THE MISSION!

IT WAS WHEN we ceased to do God's work here that we got into trouble. When our eyes fell away from God, they fell on each other and, being human, we did not like what we saw.

WHAT BEGAN as a whisper became a mighty wind. Rumors raged. Families feuded. Satan sat down on the church step and had a holiday. Our church became a warship instead of a house of worship, a battleground, instead of a blessed ground, an offense instead of an offering to God who gave us everything that we have.

OUR CHRISTIAN FATHERS faced the wilderness with sacrifice and found victory. When we begin to give of ourselves, we shall share in that victory. The beginning has been made here. You have seen it, and all of this community has taken notice. There is a people looking up to God and doing His Work.

GOD DOES NOT want our pocketbook. He wants our hands and our hearts. What profit is there if we gain all of Galion and lose our own souls?

I HAVE HEARD it said that some will not join this church, because they fear that they will be given something to do. But I also know of some people who almost left this church because they were never asked to do anything. Thank God Trinity Church has become a doing church!

OUR HORIZON is bright for 1964. We are again looking to

God for the future. We are firm in our faith. Our souls are secure. With God in our hearts and the world behind us, we will again begin to build with our hands a new church—a new community—a new and greater Trinity for the glory of God alone!

AMEN.

EVERYTHING WILL BE OKAY

January 19, 1964
   Trinity Lutheran Church, Galion, Ohio
   Second Sunday After Epiphany

On the occasion of the January Quarterly Meeting

TEXT: Psalm 34: 4-8
   "I SOUGHT THE LORD, and he answered me, and delivered me from all my fears. Look to him, and be radiant; so your faces shall never be ashamed. This poor man cried, and the Lord heard him, and saved him out of all his troubles. The angel of the Lord encamps around those who fear him, and delivers them. O taste and see that the Lord is good! Happy is the man who takes refuge in him!"
   MAJOR GORDON COOPER was on the seventeenth course of his twenty-two-orbit flight around the earth. It was the night of May 15, 1963.
   A HUNDRED MILES below him lay the Indian Ocean. A canopy of stars stretched infinite distances of eerie light above him. Overwhelmingly impressed by God's guidance as he

moved serenely through the vastness of outer space, Gordon Cooper pushed the button of his tape recorder and recorded a prayer for himself and for all who had to do with the building and launching of his spaceship.

HERE IS HIS PRAYER: "Father, thank You, especially for letting me fly this flight. Thank You for the privilege of being able to be in this position, to be up in this wondrous lace, seeing all these many startling wonderful things that you have created.

"HELP guide and direct all of us that we may shape our lives to be much better Christians, trying to help one another and to work with one another, rather than fighting and bickering. Help me to complete this mission successfully.

"HELP US in our future space endeavors, that we may show the world that a democracy can really compete and still is able to do things in a big way, and is able to do research, and can conduct many scientific and very technical problems.

"BE WITH OUR FAMILIES. Give them guidance and encouragement, and let them know that everything will be okay. We ask in Thy name. Amen."

EVERYTHING WILL BE OKAY. Yes. Major Cooper was right when he said: "Everything will be okay!"

ROBERT BROWNING sang:
"God's in his heaven—
All's right with the world."

BUT Browning was only half right. God is in His heaven, but everything in the world is not all right.

THERE IS REALLY much here that is wrong. Filthy, crowded slums. Sick people languishing without medical care. Hungry people dying without bread enough for one last meal. Travelers hideously smashed on speed haunted highways. Blind people groping for light, hearing only screams of terror. Those with half a mind are shut away. The crippled are left to hobble.

THE PICTURE of our lives is not pretty. Men and women

cheating, lying, gossiping, stealing, killing, violating innocence. Our lives are sick with the vomit of disillusionment, despair, and decay.

MANY THINGS are wrong with this world, but not all things. There is still grass waiting under the snow, and flower seeds still are alive in the frozen ground. There are sights and sounds and tastes all around us that delight the senses. You can smell the excitement of the Holy Spirit in the air that is bringing new life into Morrow County. You can smell the roast in the oven on which you will feast for Sunday dinner. We have a fine hospital in our town to care for the sick. You have brought much food to the parsonage to be given to the hungry.

ALL AROUND US there is love—the love of parents and children, of husbands and wives, of young men and young women, of a pastor and his people. There is the velvet vibration of music and the lifting laughter of children. There is respect for the flag and reverence for sacred things. Many things in this world are right.

AND MANY THINGS that are wrong become right. Hunger yields to satisfaction. Loneliness finds a friend. Pain gives way to healing. Darkness pales as a new day dawn. Ignorance gives place to knowledge and wisdom. Hatred and misunderstanding fall at the feet of love and appreciation. Out of catastrophe comes deliverance. Sin is pardoned. Evil men become instruments for good.

HERE IN OUR CONGREGATION TODAY, we can recognize the care of a loving Father within the shadows, keeping watch over His own, because He cares, because He loves us.

GOD IS GOOD. And if we pause long enough to reflect this morning, we shall discern His goodness. We shall see clearly that He has been good to us here.

THE PSALMIST WRITES: "The Angel of the Lord encamps around those who fear him, and delivers them."

THIS IS A COMFORTING MESSAGE for the present. But what of our future? What of the future of Trinity Church? Must evil versus good continue forever? Must our lives always be a mixture of right and wrong?

NO! God is in heaven. And there will come a day when heaven will encompass the earth, and wrong will be swallowed up by right. Then all will be right with the world.

AND ALL WILL BE RIGHT with us here, too! God will wipe the sorrow from our hearts. The hurt that sears our souls will be healed. The tears will dry up in our eyes. Sisters will speak to sisters again—brothers to brothers. Mothers again will be cared for by sons and daughters. Friends will be loved for what they are and not for what we would like them to be.

AND IN THIS PLACE, the face of God will shine from our faces, and the name of God will be stamped on our foreheads, and the work of God will be done by our hands.

YES, MAJOR COOPER, everything will be okay at Trinity Church. God promises it, and His Word can never fail!

AMEN.

THE CHALLENGE OF PRAYER

January 26, 1964
   Trinity Lutheran Church, Galion, Ohio
   Septuagesima Sunday

TEXT: Matthew 7:7-9
   ASK, and it will be given you; seek and you will find; knock, and it will be opened to you. For everyone who asks receives, and he who seeks finds, and to him who knocks it will be opened.
   "LET'S PRAY HARD, YOU GUYS, or this ship's going to blow up!"
   That American sailor who shouted this plea on his burning carrier during World War II told the truth about the "good ship earth," as well as for his carrier. For our wounded world is full of holes. There is fury and fire in its four corners. There are man-made explosions deep in its bowels. One more global war, and we shall all be destroyed. "Pray hard, you guys, or this ship's going to blow up!"
   PRAYER helped these gobs to keep cool heads so that they did the right things to put out the fires. Their ship still floats.

Prayer will do the same thing for us. We need cool heads to do the right thing—to put out the fires of hate and prejudice if our ship earth is to survive. Prayer will quench hate, fear, and panic when nothing else seems to work.

FRANK LAUBACH says we need to mobilize a new army of ten million and train them to use a weapon as powerful as rocket bombs were used for destruction. Other weapons convert enemies into skeletons. This weapon must convert enemies into friends. It must heal the horrid open wound that bombs have left across the face of our world.

THIS IS THE CHALLENGE OF PRAYER. Only prayer, which releases the infinite might of God, can win this final battle for men's minds and hearts—this battle against hate—this battle for "one world," one with God, peoples one with each other in peace and good will.

ENOUGH PEOPLE PRAYING long enough and hard enough will release into the world's bloodstream the mightiest medicine in our universe, for through prayer we become channels through whom God can exert his infinite power and blessing to the world.

OUR PRAYERS are to the world just what white corpuscles are to the human body. If there are not enough white corpuscles in our bloodstream, our diseased bodies remain sick and eventually die. Without proper prayer, our souls remain sick—out of tune with God. But if enough of us pray enough, there can be and there will be peace—peace of mind and heart, and peace for our time.

IF WE DO NOT PRAY—and enough like us do not pray—hell will break loose again, and we and our homes and our loved ones will be sucked into the bursting holocaust and bloody horror of another war—too horrible to comprehend—and perish.

YOU SAY, "Prayer alone will not be enough! We need right

deeds!" Precisely! Prayer without perspiration has no purpose. In fact, lately I've come to the thinking that prayer and perspiration cannot be separated. It is of little value for any of us to get down on our knees to pray if, when we get back up on our feet, we fail to roll up our sleeves and put our prayers to work. If we Christian people are not willing to work with God in the answering of our prayers, then our perfectly worded, precisely spoken prayers are not more than perfumed pipe-dreams!

JESUS SAYS, "Ask...Seek...Knock, and it will be opened for you." For us, prayer is the door that opens our minds and the minds of our leaders to God. It is through prayer that we and they come to know which deeds are right. Then God gives us the power to put those deeds to work.

"HA!" rebuked a friend. "If Prayers can save the world, why haven't the prayers of the faithful done it already?" Because our prayers have only been a trickle when we needed a river. A drop in a great big bucket.

THE WORLD TODAY is the result of the total thought forces that have struggled for supremacy. We have had all these wars because wills all over the world have been at cross purposes with the will of God and with other wills.

THE PEOPLE who were working and planning with God were fewer than those working and planning against God. We prayed for a few minutes a week when we should have been praying all week, all year, "without ceasing."

"I AM VERY SENSITIVE," a preacher once told his congregation. "I know when you are praying for me. If one of you lets me down, I feel it. When you are praying for me, I feel a strange power. When every person in a congregation prays intensely while the pastor is preaching, a miracle happens. If it does not happen today, somebody has failed to pray. Let us make it unanimous and see what happens when EVERYBODY is praying."

DR. GLENN CLARK, the greatest practitioner of prayer I

have ever known, tried this appeal once with his congregation. Almost immediately while they began to pray, he felt like he was lifted out of himself and possessed by Christ. He felt as though Christ were talking through his lips. Many others shared his experience. After the sermon, six people came to him and said: "We saw Christ standing beside you!"

AS HE WENT out of church, a woman was sobbing with her head on the seat. He sat down beside her and asked if he could help.

"I DON'T BELIEVE IN SUCH THINGS," she said, "but what can I do? I saw Christ myself!"

WHAT HAD HAPPENED? Those people had been caught by the challenge of prayer. They had been so melted into one by prayer that it had in some way enabled the Invisible Christ to become visible to about a dozen eyes.

WHAT WOULD HAPPEN HERE if we caught the challenge of prayer and put it to work? When a congregation prays in solid array, we have the same conditions they had at Pentecost. The books of Acts says, "These all continued unanimously in prayer and supplication."

LIKE RADIOS, we seem to be tuned in to each other a part of the time and turned off at other times. Can you imagine the marvelous events that would happen here, if we would all tune in on God's channel together, at the same time, one in prayer, in purpose, and in love?

OUR PRAYERS MAY SEEM WEAK AT FIRST. Prayers have a way of being disturbed. Instead of picturing Christ in prayer, we catch glimpses of the roast in the oven at home, visions of the parking meter that we cheated yesterday. We see clearly the good deed not done, the bad deed done too well. But as we pray we can feel ourselves grow in power with God.

OUR PRAYERS COME BACK TO US LIKE RADAR. When that happens, our hearts skip a beat with the thrill of it, for we know we are learning to be channels for God—working for Him in His Kingdom.

BEING CAUGHT UP IN PRAYER may be illustrated from the experience of an English pilot as he told the story of how he came to be taken prisoner during World War II.

FLYING OVER ENEMY TERRITORY, he was caught in the cone of a searchlight from the ground. No matter which way he turned—no matter what stunts he performed—he could not get out of that beam of light.

THIS IS OUR TASK in prayer. In our prayer, we hold people in the light of the Word of God, that even though they may be uncomfortable and disturbed in it, they may, nevertheless, be held until won by the love that will not let us go.

ASK! SEEK! KNOCK! The invitation to prayer is compelling. But it must be accepted or rejected. The gospel is never a calm, dispassionate account of what God has done or is doing. It is an urgent summons to act—to do—"Choose this day whom you shall serve!"

SOMEONE HAS SAID that people do not ooze into the Kingdom of God. They must choose. Failure to choose is itself a wrong choice. Facing the Word of God results in a verdict. Good or evil. Right or wrong. Heaven or hell.

THE URGENT NEED TODAY is for faithful men and women who will work and pray for God and each other. For the faithful who will brave this new world and compel others to come in. For the faithful who have caught and accepted the Challenge of Prayer.

SO I SAY TO YOU, walk back into the tomorrow of life unafraid. Go back to your work, however disappointing. Go back to your home, no matter what problems or pain are there. Go on living, no matter how disillusioned you may be.

THE FORCES OF THIS WORLD ARE DOOMED. Greed and hate have not a ghost of a chance where the faithful of God have caught the challenge of prayer. In the economy of God, love is still omnipotent, and faith is still irresistible. This way of life cannot fail.

Never you worry.
Never you fret.
God is not done
With this old world yet!
AMEN.

THE POWER OF PRAYER

February 2, 1964
Trinity Lutheran Church, Galion, Ohio
Sexagesima Sunday

TEXT: James 5:16. NEB

A GOOD MAN'S PRAYER is powerful and effective.

MANY OF THE PROBLEMS of our lives are graphically portrayed for us in the well-known story of Goldilocks. When her curiosity led her to the home of the three bears, the first thing that caught her attention were the three bowls of soup, which represented the three needs of our lives, the physical, the mental, and the spiritual.

AND IF YOU REMEMBER, those bowls were graduated in size from a big bowl you could always see to a teeny weeny one that was almost invisible.

FIRST, Goldilocks tried the big bowl, but that was too hot! Next, she tried the middle-sized bowl, but that was too cold! For Goldilocks, cold war—or war of the mind and intellect—was just as futile as the hot war of brute strength.

LAST OF ALL, Goldilocks tried the little bowl filled with

God's spirit. And it was just right. It was perfect. But woe to us all, there was not enough of it!

THIS IS HOW OUR LIVES ARE. We have the three bowls, or three sides of life, in our grasp—the physical, the mental, and the spiritual. Our largest effort goes for physical prowess and power. The next share goes for intellectual pursuits—the love of wisdom, the love of a good argument, the love of a good fight without getting our hands dirty.

THE SMALLEST share of our effort goes for the spiritual side of our lives. The littlest bowl is saved for our share for the Kingdom of God.

THIS IS WHY we need the power of prayer in our lives—to increase the size of the spiritual bowl, so there will be enough of God's power there to meet our needs and the needs of the world in which we live.

BUT WE CHRISTIANS have lost much of our spiritual power—the closeness with God that the first Christians had at the day of Pentecost. All we have to do is look around us for the evidence that the power of prayer is largely gone today.

IT IS DISHEARTENING to see the submissiveness of school boards, teachers, and public officials who are going beyond the Supreme Court edict in removing all references to God and His power from the eyes and ears of our children.

THE NEW YORK STATE Education Commissioner, for example, has declared that the fourth stanza of "America," which refers to God, cannot be used as a part of the opening exercises in schools in that state.

IN SACRAMENTO COUNTY, CALIFORNIA, it has been ruled unconstitutional for children to say this grace with their milk and cookies:

God is great.
God is good.
Let us thank Him for our food.

BEHIND THE SCENES, there are forces at work to remove God as an important source of power in our lives. Like in the Goldilocks story, the spiritual bowl in America is almost empty. Satan is pouring sour milk on the few grains of good that are clinging to the bottom of the bowl.

BILLY GRAHAM was right when he said in his recent Los Angeles Crusade, "The effort to remove God and moral teachings from our schools is a diabolical scheme." It is the devil's work, but it is working! For the most part, Christians have lost sight of the power of prayer everywhere. And prayer without power has no purpose. So why not let them take it away?

LET US TAKE A REALISTIC LOOK at history. The philosophy of our nation has been the "survival of the fittest." Due to the blindness of our leaders, this has been perverted to mean the survival of the "best fitted fighter." Those most adept in destroying the lives of others without being destroyed themselves.

OPPOSED to this modern philosophy is the completely contrasting philosophy of Jesus: "The meek shall inherit the earth!"

THERE WE HAVE IT. "The survival of the fittest." "The meek shall inherit the earth." Let us see which one has won the verdict of history.

ARE THERE ANY dinosaurs, saber-toothed tigers, or cavebears today? Not only have they become extinct, but gorillas and grizzlies are gradually slipping away. Lions and tigers are fading away.

THE CREATURES that are surviving in vast numbers are not the powerful beasts that brought terror to the earth, but the helpless cattle and sheep—those creatures that are by character MEEK, those creatures that SERVE.

WE, TOO, WILL BECOME EXTINCT if we do not learn how to serve. There is no better way to serve God than to tune in on his power and then to use that power to work His will in this world.

"PRAYER IS SOMETHING THE PASTOR DOES," I always thought—until I became a Pastor and found out that prayer is something that the people do better.

A SMALL GROUP of praying people need not wait for an invitation from the pastor or for the rest of the congregation. They can band themselves together in prayer. And if they persist long enough and earnestly enough, they will set the church on fire. This kind of prayer is hard work, but the spiritual rewards are wonderful.

A SMALL PRAYER GROUP is forming in our congregation. Have you been spiritually alert enough to know about it? Do you care enough to join?

PRAYER LIKE THAT HAS POWER. Where two or three are gathered in the name of Christ, He is there!

CHRIST SAYS, "Behold I stand at the door and knock." But God cannot get in, for most of us have the door of our hearts closed to Him nearly all of the time. Many of us have lost the key. Some never talk to God. We will listen to each other a million times before we will listen to God. The telephone rings! We will get on the party line, but we stay off of the power line— that private line between us and God! Our thoughts are purely personal, hardly ever prayerful, and positively not powerful. Lost from our lives is the power from prayer that God has promised.

MILLIONS AND MILLIONS have prayed through the last war that their sons, husbands, and brothers would return whole. That is good, but prayer should not end with the present problem. Prayer is too small when it ends with our families or friends or even with our own country.

"BRING my boy home alive and well. Save us from sin and

danger. God bless America! If I should die before I wake, I pray the Lord my soul to take." These prayers are good, but too small.

AN AUTOMOBILE needs a constant stream of gasoline to give it power. If that stream of gasoline is obstructed in any way, the engine sputters and stops. Our spiritual lives dilly-dally and die when we dangle hopelessly at the end of a broken line of prayerful communication with God. He is the source of our power. Our spiritual cup must never be found empty.

THIS WOULD COME OUT RIGHT if only we would pray. There is where we are powerful. To be alarmed, or plunged into despair, or to scold—all that is futile. It only makes matters worse. Our world already is in a bad humor.

BUT WHEN we organize a prayer army, we gain a tremendous power with God. Desperately eager people would pray if they knew prayer could save them. They are waiting for us to lead the way.

THE MOST TRAGIC MISTAKE we can make is to ignore God's power and his claims on our lives until it is everlastingly too late.

HERE IS OUR PRAYER: "Our power comes from Thee, O Lord; Forward is the only way we can go! AMEN!"

CHRIST SHOW US THE WAY

February 9, 1964
    Trinity Lutheran Church, Galion, Ohio
    Quinquagesima Sunday

TEXT: 1 Corinthians 1:22-31

JEWS CALLS FOR MIRACLES, Greeks look for wisdom; but we proclaim Christ—yes, Christ nailed to the cross; and though this is a stumbling-block to Jews and folly to Greeks, yet to those who have heard his call, Jews and Greeks alike, he is the power of God and the wisdom of God.

Divine folly is wiser than the wisdom of man, and divine weakness stronger than man's strength. My brothers, think what sort of people you are, whom God has called. Few of you are men of wisdom by any human standard. Few are powerful or highly born. Yet to shame the wise, God has chosen things low and contemptible, mere nothings, to overthrow the existing order. And so there is no place for human pride in the presence of God. You are in Christ Jesus by God's Act, for God made him our wisdom. He is our righteousness. In him we are consecrated and set free. And so, in the words of scripture, "If a man is proud, let him be proud of the Lord."

THERE IS ONE VICE of which not one of us is free. One vice that everyone in the world loathes when he sees it in someone else and that hardly any people ever imagine they are guilty of themselves.

I HAVE HEARD people admit they are ill-tempered, that they cannot keep their heads about gossiping or drinking, or that they are cowards. But I do not think I have ever heard anyone who was not a Christian accuse himself of *this* vice.

THE VICE I am talking about is pride or self-centeredness. There is no fault that makes us more unpopular, and no fault that we are more unconscious of in ourselves than *pride*. And the more we have it ourselves, the more we dislike it in others.

PRIDE is the essential vice, the utmost vice. Unchastity, anger, greed, drunkenness, and all the rest are mere fleabites by comparison. It was through pride that the Devil became the Devil. Pride leads to every other vice we could mention. It is the complete anti-God state of mind.

FROM CHILDHOOD until the hour we draw our last breath, one of the worst enemies of our health and well-being, and of our ability to contribute to the health and well-being of others, is the temptation to self-pride, self-worship, and even self-pity. These are more subtle forms of Pride.

SOME UNKNOWN WRITER has given us these practical suggestions on "How To Be Absolutely Miserable."

Think about yourself.

Talk about yourself. Use "I" as often as possible.

Mirror yourself continually in the opinion of others.

Listen greedily to what people say about you.

Expect to be appreciated.

Be jealous and envious.

Be sensitive to slights.

Never forgive a criticism.

Trust nobody but yourself.

Insist on consideration and respect.

Sulk if people are not grateful for favors shown them.

Love yourself supremely!

IT IS GOD'S PLAN that we center our lives on him alone. Pride cannot bear this kind of competition. It cuts us off from God. Pride has been the chief cause of misery in every nation and every family since the world began. Other vices plague us for a while, but pride always means enmity. It *is* enmity. And not only enmity between brother and brother, sister and sister, but enmity between us and God!

MARTIN LUTHER once said, "If anyone raps at the door of my heart and says: 'Who lives here?' I say Martin Luther used to. But he moved out and Jesus Christ moved in."

OUR HEARTS may be filled or controlled by three forces: our self, Satan, or God. There is not room for all three at the same time. In fact, there is room for only one of them at a time. We have to choose between our self, Satan, or God.

IN GOD, we come up against something that is in every respect immeasurably superior to ourselves. Unless we know God as that—and know ourselves as nothing in comparison— we do not know God at all. As long as we are proud, we cannot know God. A proud man is always looking down on things and people. And of course, as long as we are looking down, we cannot look up. We cannot see God!

SPEAKING THROUGH the Prophet Jerimiah, God warns us, "Let not the wise man glory in his wisdom, let not the mighty man glory in his might, let not the rich man glory in his riches; but let him who glories glory in this, that he understands and knows me."

PAUL WARNS US that what we have or what we have done

in the past are not the ultimate. Rather, to find God through Christ should be our goal.

PAUL PUT IT THIS WAY: "If any man be in Christ, he is a new creature: old things are passed away; behold all things become new." That is the essence of the glad Christian gospel. We do not have to stay the way we are! To find Christ is the answer for a full and rich life.

WE KNOW NO WORDS that can define the Lord Jesus Christ. Like the Corinthians of our text, we can neither find nor come to know him through our own wisdom or mental ability. This bothered the Jews and Greeks of Paul's time, who were proud of their education, proud of what they had built, proud of their logical minds.

RECOGNIZING the source of their spiritual blindness, Paul called pride their stumbling block. To both the Jew and the Greek, the cross of Christ was not a product of wisdom, not logical—in fact, a stumbling block. The cross was to them a sign of weakness, not of strength and salvation.

BUT TO US CHRISTIANS whom God calls, the cross is both power and wisdom that can destroy pride and selfishness once and forever!

PAUL TURNED THE TABLES on the selfish Corinthians by reminding them that their own call to build their church was proof of God's resourceful wisdom in Christ.

LIKE THE EARLY CHRISTIANS, few of us have any title to worldly respect by reason of our knowledge, influence, or birth. Yet we have been selected by God to carry out his sovereign plan. We have been selected by God to build his church.

FEW MEN of distinction were found among the storekeepers, tentmakers, laborers, slaves, and free men who formed the membership of the early church. Few men of distinction are found here in Trinity Lutheran Church. Yet every one of us has been called here by God to build his church.

IF IT IS THE NATURE of a tree to bear sour apples, all you can get from that tree is sour apples. No matter how abundant the fruit may be. No matter how beautiful its color or form. It is sour. You must change the nature of that tree before it will bear good fruit.

ONLY THOSE WHO forget themselves and stand in a right relation with God will help to build his church. Without God, we are by character "sour apples." We must allow him to change us before any real good can be done.

WE DARE NOT let the past or our pride prevent us from doing God's work. Centered in Christ—made secure by the cross—our future is uncertain. It is now time for us to pick up the bricks and start to build.

AMEN.

WHAT DOES THE CROSS MEAN TO ME?

February 12, 1964
   Ash Wednesday Service of Holy Communion
   Trinity Lutheran Church, Galion, Ohio

TEXT: 1 John 1:5-9

HERE IS THE MESSAGE we heard from him and pass on to you: that God is light, and in him there is no darkness at all. If we claim to be sharing in his life while we walk in the dark, our words and our lives are a lie; but if we walk in the light as he himself is in the light, then we share together a common life, and we are being cleansed from every sin by the blood of Jesus Christ.

TODAY IS ASH WEDNESDAY—the first day of Lent. Today, we begin a sad season in the life of the Christian. It is forty days long. It is beginning early this year. For those of us who traditionally try to give up something for Lent, it will seem even longer.

DURING LENT, a ball drops over the Christian Church. This is symbolized by the veil on our cross. The cross is not hidden. The cross is still there. The veil reminds us to ask the question, "What does the cross of Jesus Christ mean to me?"

LENT IS A TIME for serious soul-searching. We look up to Christ for our coming salvation. But during Lent, we look inside ourselves to see if we are ready to accept His salvation when it comes.

THE DARKNESS of the agony and travail of Jesus Christ is all around us. He died because of our sin. We live because he died. That is the truth of the glad Christian gospel.

OFTEN, I HAVE TRAVELED along the Pennsylvania Turnpike. If you have ever traveled this road, perhaps you remember the many tunnels you encounter when driving through Philadelphia.

APPROACHING a tunnel, you see warning signs along the high-speed highway. "Tunnel Ahead! Slow Down! One Lane Traffic! Turn On Your Lights!"

IN AN INSTANT, you are inside the tunnel, enveloped in darkness, the roaring of motors, and confusion. You are in there, you know you are moving forward, but there seems no end, no way out.

THEN in the distance you see a pinpoint of light. That light grows slowly larger as you approach the end of the long, dark tunnel. It is a glorious thing to watch the tunnel exit loom larger and larger as you rush toward it.

ALL OF A SUDDEN you can see that the sun is shining outside. The sun is shining and all is well with the world, and you soon will be there.

LEAVING THE TUNNEL BEHIND, I always seemed to enjoy the fresh air and the flowers a bit more than when I entered. It is not that there were no flowers or fresh air on the other side of the hill. It is just that I always appreciate things more when I do not have them for a little while.

HOW OFTEN I have walked across a field going to a definite

place at a definite time, completely ignoring the grass under my feet.

HOW MUCH MORE we will appreciate the victory of the cross when the veil comes off this Easter morning because it was hidden for a while. This is why we celebrate Lent in the Christian Church. Lent is like going through a long, dark tunnel. We rush into it on Ash Wednesday, and suddenly we are aware as we look at ourselves of the walls of life pushing in on us, aware of the darkness that envelopes our world because of sin.

THE WARNING SIGNS are everywhere. "Watch out! Take care of your soul! You may die before you wake!"

BUT LOOK! In the distance is the light of Jesus Christ! Like in the tunnel, His light may seem small at first, but as we purge ourselves, clean ourselves out and let Him in, His light will become a larger force in our lives.

AS WE APPROACH the great light of Easter this year, we will know that the sun is shining because of the victory of Jesus Christ. We will be better Christians because we have walked this road. We will be better Christians, because to walk toward Christ is walking His road.

EVERY TIME we enter this church during these forty days and look at the cross of Jesus Christ, let us ask ourselves this question, "What does the cross of Jesus Christ mean to me?"

AMEN.

SAVED TO SERVE

February 16, 1964
 Trinity Lutheran Church, Galion, Ohio
 Invocabit: Second Sunday In Lent

TEXT: 2 Corinthians 6:11-13
 "OUR MOUTH is open to you, Corinthians; our heart is wide. You are not restricted by us, but you are restricted in your own affections. In return—I speak as to children—widen your hearts also."
 WALLS OF CONCRETE, barbed wire, watch-towers, searchlights, and tall prisons. We do not expect to find these in America. Rather, these are foreign, totalitarian, and most certainly under suspicion. Yet many of us who are law-abiding citizens in a free nation and even freer community are busy building prisons for ourselves. Every day, we shut ourselves off a little more from the outside world, block by block we make the walls around us a little higher and a little thicker. The mortar holding these self-built walls is an awesome mixture of fear, frustration, and folly.

EVERY PRISON HAS CELLS—even the prison of life, which we have built. We call these self-built cells by curious names, and they all keep us from the kind of Christian service that is necessary to save this world.

ONE OF THESE CELLS is "Self-Disparagement." Standing securely behind the shadow of this selfish wall that we have built up around us, hoping that nobody can peer over, and glad that we are blinded and cannot see out, some of us spend all of our energy cutting ourselves apart into bloody little pieces.

THESE are the Christians who do not feel that they can do anything right. They would like to work in the Church, but they do not feel qualified. They would like to call on the sick, but they do not have clothes good enough to wear, or there is too much lint on their best suit. They would go to a Bible Study, but they might get nervous, or it might rain, or they might make a mistake reading the Bible, or someone might say something that would offend.

CHRISTIANS WHO LIVE in this self-built cell might get into heaven, but I doubt if they will ever do anything for Christ here on earth. They are too busy chewing on their own hearts, watching themselves bleed and die inside, to care about anything else.

ANOTHER CELL is "Over-Criticalness." The Christian who builds this kind of prison for himself or herself builds just a little bit higher than everyone else. And there they sit—way up there—out of the spotlight—a little bit in the shadow.

FROM THEIR VANTAGE POINT, they can see the worst in everyone and call it down quietly so that it echoes from the four corners of the church, but nobody really knows from where it comes. Instead of a help, it is more like a hiss: "He is nice, but... The new hymnals are pretty, but... I'd give more to the building fund, but..."

OH, SAINT PETER will probably let these "Over-Critical Christians" by the gate, BUT... But what on earth have they ever accomplished on earth?

ANOTHER CELL in the prison of life is "Chronic Worry." For the chronic worrier, the picture of the future is already painted, and it is all black—black as coal, jet black, with not one ray of light or hope anywhere. These Christians have selfishly blinded themselves to what can be done in the present and projected themselves into a hopelessly bleak and foreboding future.

AS CHRONIC WORRIERS, we have gotten ourselves into such a state that many of us are merely pounding our heads against a concrete wall, hoping against hope that we will feel better when we stop. This does not leave us much time for the business of serving Christ. Having not enough faith for the present, we stand and fritter away our future.

"DWELLING IN THE PAST" is a cell, too. These Christians see "the good old days" and "the good old ways" as golden. In fact, so brightly does the past shine in the memory that the present work is blotted out.

THE PAST has been our teacher, but the present is our mission field. We must re-direct our energies from "what was" to "what is." We dare not let down those pastors who came here and prayed, and sweat, and walked the floors many a lonely night to find an answer out of trouble so that Trinity Lutheran Church might grow and serve. The past has been good here, but it only has a purpose in so far as we perfect the future. And the only way we can do this is by serving Christ.

ENVY: There is a cell with walls made out of the hardest stuff. God's love rarely can penetrate these walls, but our hands can get out and grab and hoard. It is the envious Christian that covets. He or she is like a child who is so excited about getting his fair share of cake and icing that he scoops his piece out of the middle with his hands and ruins the cake for everyone. When we fall to envy, we become so concerned about what others have or are getting that we cannot see the good we already have for ourselves. We grab and hold everything so tightly that we forget how to give. We demand service, but forget how to serve!

THERE IS ONE CELL in the prison of life that always has a locked door. It is located at the end of the darkest and deepest dungeon. It is self-made too; but it has a professional touch to it. The door is locked, but it is an attractive door. There are even some geraniums budding from an inviting planter. No one who has ever ventured down that dark hallway ever comes back without a knife in the back.

IN A STRAWBERRY COLOR, a neon sign flashes—HATE! Hate! Those who live in this cell rarely come out. Because of what they have done, they fear what people will say. They spend most of their time sticking pins in people and projects. They sow the seeds of evil and wrap them up in the most beautiful packages you can imagine.

THE PRISON OF LIFE... It has many cells, and they all have a name: Self-Disparagement. Over-Criticalness. Chronic Worry. Dwelling in the Past. Envy. Hate.

THE NAME OF THE PRISON? SIN! Many a Christian is trapped there—in the prison of sin. "Pride" is the jailer that keeps us locked in. And when we lock ourselves in, we have locked God out. Preoccupied with ourselves, we do not do God's will in the world.

THERE IS A KEY! There is one key that can open all of the doors. That key is prayer. But we must be honestly humble to use it.

GOD HAS A MUCH BETTER FUTURE planned for us than this. The embryo of a dog will always become a dog. The process can never go wrong. But is it equally certain that a human embryo will become a man? It may become "inhuman."

WE CAN let ourselves grow to be entirely different from what God intended for our lives. We can become "spiritual renegades"—constantly sabotaging the plans of God for our lives, wasting our talents, throwing away our destiny—until eventually we end up in the pigpen with the Prodigal Son.

THIS is not only possible, but precisely what happens to us when we wall up our lives to suit ourselves and leave God out of the picture.

IT IS THE WILL OF GOD that we become concerned about all of those around us, that we do not build up any barrier around our hearts—or at our church door—that would prevent us from offering a helping hand to those who have no church, or bringing home those who have no Savior. Every wall we build up is an offense to God.

ROBERT FROST put it this way in his poem "The Mending Wall."

Something there is that doesn't love a wall,
That sends the frozen-ground-swell under it...
Before I built a wall, I'd ask to know
What I was walling in or walling out,
And to whom I was like to give offense.
Something there is that doesn't love a wall—
THAT WANTS IT DOWN.

WALT WHITMAN once wrote, "Not till the sun refuses you do I refuse you!" Here is the spirit of the Christian Church. Not until the Son of God refuses us dare we ever refuse to serve those who are in need. We have been saved so that we might serve. Our service, and only our service, should be the measure of our concern.

Tear down the walls! God made of one
All men who live upon the earth;
God is our Creator, we God's children
Whatsoever be our human birth.
AMEN.

FORGIVEN, LET US FORGIVE

February 23, 1964
  Trinity Lutheran Church, Galion, Ohio
  Reminiscere: Third Sunday in Lent

TEXT: 1 John 1:5-10

THIS IS THE MESSAGE we have heard from him and proclaim to you, that God is light and in God is no darkness at all. If we say we have fellowship with God while we walk in darkness, we lie and do not live according to the truth; but if we walk in the light, as God is in the light, we have fellowship with one another, and the blood of Jesus, God's Child, cleanses us from all sin. If we say we have no sin, we deceive ourselves, and the truth is not in us. If we confess our sins, God is faithful and just, and will forgive our sins and cleanse us from all unright-eousness. If we say we have not sinned, we make God a liar, and God's word is not in us.

DURING my early college years, before I acquired an auto-mobile, I did most of my traveling on the Greyhound bus. I recall one day I was sitting in a bus in a single seat over one of the rear wheels, slightly above everyone else, in such a way that I could see the hands and faces of my fellow passengers.

ONE MAN carried an unsightly scar on his right hand. It was ugly and red, crisscrossing the entire length of the back of his hand. The stitch marks were purple and had not entirely healed. Instinctively, the man would either hold his scarred hand in the pocket of his coat or hide it under the newspaper he was reading.

THEN I BEGAN TO LOOK for scars. They were not hard to find. Another man was severely crippled. His heavy braces would not permit him to sit comfortably in the cramped quarters of the old bus. Then there was the woman with her arm in a cast. The little boy with a patch over his right eye. The little girl with the club foot.

IF THERE WERE so many exposed wounds, I thought to myself, there must be many more unexposed. I began to look for evidence of wounded minds and spirits. There were twitches in the cheeks, furrows on the brows, black rings around eyes, painful movements of hands and feet.

I OBSERVED in some what seemed to be indications of illness—coughs, blowing noses, sneezes. I descended from the bus at the Pittsburgh terminal with one thought—EVERYBODY'S WOUNDED!

THE UNIVERSALITY OF WOUNDS! "In this world you have tribulation," said Jesus. Tribulation. The tribulum was a Roman threshing instrument. It was made out of spikes driven through boards. This instrument was then pulled over the wheat harvested in the stalk and spread out on the threshing floor. It would release the grain from the hulls, but it would not bruise the wheat. On the Cross, Jesus Christ was bruised by the tribulation of this world.

WHERE IS THE PERSON who has not been bruised by the tribulum of this world? The horrible spiked boards of life?

Where is the person who has not seen tribulation? Everybody's bruised. Look at this morning's newspaper. Whole people and races are bruised. Nations carry the scars of war and of tyranny. Tyrannies have crushed millions of people—common people trying with all of the force within their control to get ahead, just like us here this morning.

THE DOWNTRODDEN bear wounds on their hearts and eat mud. Refugees have wounded memories. Whole populations are in poverty. There is an epidemic of fever in our world. It was for a world like ours that Christ came to the Cross. It was for people like us that he faced the depravity of physical need. "I thirst."

A STORY BY GENE BARTLETT comes out of those hungry days after World War II. One relief worker tells of going into a war area and holding a glass of milk before a child whose eyes seemed much bigger because of the gauntness of his little face.

REMEMBERING the days past when all of his many brothers and sisters had to drink from the same cup, the child held the glass in his weak and shaking hands and asked: "How deep shall I drink, ma'am?" The worker was so profoundly moved by this simple and revealing question that she replied, "Drink as deep as you can, son. As deep as you can!"

NOT ONE OF US HERE THIS MORNING is starving for a glass of milk or for a crust of bread. There is not one of us here this morning who cannot say, "I have drunk deeply of all of the material things of this life." But it is quite another question to ask how deeply we should go in our faith—how far we should go to forgive others. On the Cross, Jesus showed us how far God was willing to go. We need not starve spiritually, for the Grace of God knows no exhaustion or limit. God's answer for us clearly is this: "Drink as deep as you can, sons and daughters, for my Grace is sufficient for your forgiveness."

WE HAVE BEEN FORGIVEN! No matter what scars we have

to carry through life—no matter what scars we have caused others to carry through life—God clearly has forgiven us! God has taken what was bruised, and out of that caked and clotted blood of many bleeding hearts, he has freely given HOPE and a NEW LIFE. He has turned sorrow into joy—agony and heartache into the "peace that passes all understanding."

EVERYBODY'S WOUNDED! This is true of each one of us. Many are wounded, because WE have wounded them! Our selfishness and sin crucified Jesus Christ. Our sins—pride, anger, greed, gluttony, and lust—inflict wounds that destroy lives other than our own. Why is it that we who know the forgiveness of Christ find it so difficult to forgive? Why must man show so much inhumanity to man? Why must Christians show so little forgiveness to those who are seeking Christ?

WALTER RAUSCHENBUSCH tells of a Mennonite farmer who shipped milk to Toronto. He received his empty cans back marked with a red label, indication that the milk had been poured out because it was dirty. When he saw the scarlet mark on his cans, this brother forgot the vows of his sect and swore an "unscriptural oath."

AS A RESULT of this incident, he was brought before his church, given a hearing, found guilty, and excommunicated. But he was not excommunicated for selling dirty milk. The major sin in the eyes of his ecclesiastical clansmen was not the endangering of human life through the selling of dirty milk. This was a matter of no concern for them. The moral breach for which he was tried and found guilty was the "unscriptural oath."

We Christians sometimes forget in our daily living what Christianity is all about. The forgiveness of Christ has come too easy for many of us. We hide behind the fact that we faithfully come to church and Sunday School, that we belong to a circle, that we support that church with our time and money. We hide behind the security that our sins are forgiven. Jesus Christ bore the burden of our sins to Calvary so that we might never have to bear them alone. But for many of us, the freedom of Christ's forgiveness has turned to folly! He bore our sins. This is true. But many of us will not bear anything. We cannot even bear each other! We have been forgiven by Christ, but we do not forgive.

EACH ONE OF US knows many people who have been bruised and wounded by the horrors of this world. Some of them have been so hurt that they do not know how to do anything but hate, even though they sincerely want to love. Some of them even go to church, hoping to find forgiveness there. Christ forgives them! But Christian people do not!

OFTENTIMES, when people we know are hungering and thirsting for a way out of their guilt and frustration, we who know the way will not let them have it. How would you feel, when you come to the Cross of Christ with your guilt and your sin and ask forgiveness, if he turned his back and said, "Not on your life. You're not going to get off that easy!"

"NOT ON YOUR LIFE. YOU'RE NOT GOING TO GET OFF THAT EASY!" How often we have said this to a friend who is thirsting for our forgiveness. People do not measure up to what we think they ought to be, and we cannot bear it, so we close the door! We refuse them our friendship. We refuse them our Christ. And we sit secure in our church, gloating over the fact that they are not here, supporting that they are too ashamed to come. Well, I'm ashamed to come today and to stand near the Cross of Christ and know that he suffered for me.

WHEN WE DO NOT FORGIVE as Christ as forgiven us, we frustrate our friends who are seeking a way out. Darkness becomes deeper. Hurt turns to hate. People perish. Souls are lost. A Christian congregation that does not practice forgiveness falls apart and dies.

We need dozens of people who are willing to forget their

own frustrations and fears, who are willing to forgive and bring others to Christ, who understands physical suffering. The Christian Church needs dedicated men and women like the Blue Angels. I have always viewed the idea of angels with some suspicion. It was not until the other day that I heard about "Blue Angels."

YOU CAN FIND THEM in the White Mountains of New Hampshire. They are the men who, on terrifically cold and snowy nights, patrol the notches and highways of New Hampshire in special cars with blinking blue lights. On such nights, some cars get stranded. Still others get lost.

THE BLUE ANGELS carry tow ropes, food, hot coffee, first-aid equipment, and extra gasoline. If you ever have to drive in that country in a bitter and snowy night, it is comforting to know that a Blue Angel is waiting down the road to give you help if you need it.

WE MUST BECOME BLUE ANGELS for our town—ready to bring the forgiveness of Christ to those who want it and need it, whatever the sacrifice or cost to ourselves. It is still a new year and a new road lies ahead. We can rest assured that we will meet someone in trouble soon. WE HAVE BEEN FORGIVEN. LET US FORGIVE!

AMEN.

GRANDFATHER'S GOOSE

March 1, 1964
 Trinity Lutheran Church, Galion, Ohio
 Oculi Sunday

TEXT: Ephesians 5:8
 FOR ONCE you were darkness, but now you are light in the Lord; walk as children of light.

MY GRANDFATHER once told me a story about a goose that I laughed at and quickly forgot. I did not think about it again until I read the same story in a book by Sam Gamble.

GRANDFATHER makes the claim that if you trace on a bare floor a heavy chalk circle, and you place a plain-ordinary goose inside that circle, no inducement can get the goose to cross that chalk line. My grandfather told me that the goose will starve inside the circle—starve to death in sight of food—but will not cross that chalk mark.

"I DON'T BELIEVE IT!" I told my Grandfather with the certainty that only a child of ten could have. "Nothing that breathes is quite that dumb!"

"WELL, I DON'T KNOW," the old man replied. "Geese have

very little sense. If the goose will not cross the chalk mark, it thereby proves that it is a goose."

AND THAT WAS THAT! I thought little about the intelligence quotient of geese until a farmer friend of mine in the seminary told me of how every November on their farm in Indiana they had to go out every morning with hatchets and chop dead geese out of the frozen mud of the barnyard. The barnyard is where the corn was thrown to the geese in the early evening for their daily bread. After they were fed, they just stood there and waited for more—waited until their feet froze in the mud and they died!

THERE ARE MANY HUMAN GEESE. Many of us live within the chalk line of senseless customs and conventions. When this happens, we become bogged down and become slaves to the "little laws of life."

I HAVE ALWAYS been amazed at the number of people who worship Emily Post. Even more than Ann Landers, or Norman Vincent Peale, or Saint Paul. If Emily post says DO IT, it is done!

FOR INSTANCE, Emily Post has decreed that a woman does not wear white shoes or white accessories after September 1. Yet some of our hottest weather in Ohio often comes after that date. The proper thing to wear after September 1, I am told by my wife, is Autumn colors—red, brown, dark green, and orange. These are the colors that collect and hold heat in rather than reflect it, as do the brighter colors of Spring and Summer.

HOW WILLING we are to suffer to be sociable—to sweat for society—to pay homage to Emily Post.

SOME OF MY FRIENDS have voiced concern that even during the most bitter and cold days of winter, I never wear a hat. I have a hat. I think it is a nice hat. But if I wore my hat, people would throw rocks at my head.

CUSTOM has decreed that a minister's hat should be a black or dark grey homburg with a medium band around it, a neat crease down the middle, and the brim should be worn down, pointing to the bridge of the nose.

NOW MY HAT is light grey, made out of soft fur, and it looks like it just escaped from Siberia and might bite you if disturbed. It keeps my head warm and I like it. But I do not wear it much because, as one of my classmates confided in me last winter, "It really is not a fitting thing for a minister to wear!" So I don't wear my hat!

HEREBY, I have proven that I have degenerated into a goose that has refused to step over the line.

MOST OF US LIVE within a chalk line of one kind or another. Some of us live within the chalk line of intolerance. We not only draw a line that holds us in, but a strong enough line that it holds everyone else out. We cannot tolerate some of the things that our brothers and sisters and friends do or say—so we do not tolerate them at all! Placing the chip of pride on our shoulder, we draw a line in the dust of our crumbling families and call out, "All right, brother! All right, sister! I dare you! Step over the line!"

HUMAN LOVE that is frustrated like this dies a little each day. And after a while, our brothers, sisters, and friends no longer come around. We find ourselves lost and alone. Trapped in our own trap!

OUR INTOLERANCE not only shuts out the love of our family and friends, but it also shuts out the love of Christ that can bring peace of heart and put happiness back into our lives. When we shut ourselves in, we shut Him out! Then we know the deep darkness of despair and the inner ugliness of intolerance. What a goose we become!

EDWIN MARKHAM in four lines describes a goose of this sort:

He drew a circle that shut me out,
And cried: Heretic, rebel, a thing to flout;

But love and I had the wit to win,
For we drew a bigger circle that took him in!

WHEN OTHERS BUILD A WALL around themselves to shut us out—when they are intolerant of our views or anything else about us—we must allow the love of Christ to help our arms grow wide enough to encompass them, wall and all. This is the way families are saved, souls are saved, and the love of Christ moves forward in our lives.

SOME OF US LIVE inside another chalk line—the chalk line of selfishness. Selfishness is unique. It always destroys us. My favorite illustration of "selfishness" comes out of a children's book called *The Mean Mouse and Other Mean Stories.*

THE MEAN MOUSE was just a little bit bigger than all of the other mice. He always got the biggest piece of cheese, the softest bed, and was so selfish he would not share the extra slice of bread. And he even pushed the little mice away from the line in front of the water fountain. Because of his selfishness, he grew much larger than all of the other mice.

ONE DAY, the Mean Cat sat around the corner and watched the mice as they played. As he watched, he got hungry. He licked his chops. And of course, he hate the biggest mouse.

HENRY DRUMMOND used to say of the selfish man:
He lives for himself, and he thinks of himself—
Of himself and none beside;
Just as if Jesus never lived,
And as if He never died!

THERE WAS NO selfish chalk line around the life of Jesus. He carried our sins with Him to Calvary. On the cross, He died for our sins, and not for us alone, but for the whole world. When we study his attitude toward every person with whom he came into contact and make that same attitude of love and devotion ours, any chalk line of intolerance or selfishness will vanish out of our lives.

MY MOTHER would blush if she heard me say this. I was not always a good boy at home. What little boy is? Often Mother would say: "Billy, you'd better walk the chalk line!"

IS THIS NOT WHAT we are all supposed to do? Walk the chalk line of Christianity? The chalk line of Christianity chooses for us the right goal in life. That line leads to Christ!

WHY MUST WE CONTINUE to starve ourselves spiritually like silly geese, when we know the way to salvation is Jesus Christ? Can we not let him chop us out of the mud of our lives so we can move at his call?

WE ARE NOT GEESE. We are God's!

AMEN.

THE SUNSHINE OF CHRIST

March 8, 1964
   Trinity Lutheran Church
   Laetare

Girl Scout Sunday.

TEXT: Revelation 21: 23-25
   AND THE CITY had no need of sun or moon to shine upon it; for the glory of God gave it light and its lamp was the Lamb. By its light shall the nations walk, and the kings of the earth shall bring into it all their splendor. The gates of the city shall never be shut by day—and there will be no night.
   BEWARE THE "IDES OF MARCH!"
   THIS IS A DISCOURAGING time of the year for all of us. The days are dreary, they drag, and there is little if any warmth and sunshine to bring us out of the dumps. This is a difficult period for children too—the long, colorless weeks between Christmas and Easter. There is uncertainty everywhere. The weather changes constantly—one day rain, the next day snow.

We can see the lawn again, but the only part that shows any life or health are the weeds.

AFTER EASTER, we tend to look forward to spring and summer with all of their foliage and fun. But in the early weeks of March, we get caught in the winter web of gloom, and we go about looking for trouble.

THIS IS THE TIME of the year that "pet peeves" seem to most get on our nerves. Some years ago, Professor Carson of the University of Rochester researched what peeves mankind the most. Altogether, he discovered 507 types of peeves. The professor then established a scale that ranged from 30 points— the ultimate annoyance—down to zero. The least peeve, according to Professor Carson, is seeing the bald head of a man —two points! The biggest peeve is a dirty bed. Now those peeves bother me very little. Some of my best friends have little or no hair on their heads, and by the time I get to bed, I am so tired that I could sleep soundly on burlap sacks and hay.

WHAT PEEVES ME THE MOST is the person who looks over my shoulder at the book or paper that I am reading. This must annoy others too. Curiosity is a disease! I'll never forget the day I got the cure.

IT WAS ON A CROWDED GREYHOUND bus and I was reading over the shoulder of a friend his copy of the *US News and World Report*. My friend glanced at me in disgust, but when determined, I persist. Deftly he took the magazine, found the center, and tore it in half. Giving me half, he said, "There! Now we can both read in peace!" You know? I haven't read over anyone's shoulder since!

OTHER PEEVES that bother me are a gushing manner, the sight of a snake, finding hair or a fingernail in the food I am eating, criticizing, cockroaches, flies—flies in the winter are more irritating than in the middle of summer.

THERE IS SOMETHING that annoys each one of us—and for some strange reason, this is the time of the year when those peeves become acute. If there are "people days" like there are "dog days," then the early weeks of March are "people days!"

WHAT ANNOYS US IS AN important question. Is it self-pity? Disrespect? Arguing? People crowding in front instead of waiting in line? If these are our peeves, we need not go far to become annoyed.

A MORE IMPORTANT QUESTION is "What Annoys God?" In a powerful piece of writing, Victor Hugo said many years ago, "Napoleon annoyed God, and the logical outcome was Waterloo." Saul of Tarsus annoyed God by persecuting. Peter annoyed God by thoughtless impulsiveness. Diotrephes annoyed God by posing as a church boss.

YOU AND I MAY ANNOY GOD, and God's Christ in similar ways. I imagine we annoy God most of all by our lack of a vital faith in these weary and worn days of winter.

IN COLLEGE, we always called this time of year "a grind." Anyone who has ever turned the heavy wheel of a grindstone knows what a "grind" is. Ben Franklin tells us about turning the grindstone. The story is a familiar one. A strange man who had a dull and heavy axe to grind lured the boy, Franklin, into the task of turning the stone by soft and honeyed flattery. He was "my fine fellow" while he was turning the stone. "A thoughtful and considerate boy!"

BUT WHEN the work was done at the cost of aching arms and back on Franklin's part, there was a swift change on the part of the man. Instead of giving the boy something for his labor, the man rasped the words: "Here, you little rascal, you're playing hooky! Scud off to school, or you'll rue it!"

FROM that time on, Franklin's philosophy was this: "Beware of the man who has an axe to grind."

WHY IS IT that during this time of the year, we always have an axe to grind, when turning the grindstone is our Christian duty? I can still see the grindstone that my grandfather kept outside the cellar door of his house, with its heavy sandstone wheel and the half of rubber tire that kept it wet when it was turned. The old grindstone stood under the big Catalpa tree near the smokehouse. (I learned the big word "catalpa" at college. When I was a boy, we called it the Tobey Tree, because of the long cigar-like pods it bore which you could dry out and smoke—once you could smoke one!)

THE GRINDSTONE was idle most of the year. I doubt if it was used more than a dozen days in the 365—but those few days made a world of difference in the efficiency of the axes, scythes, brush hooks, and corn-chopping knives used on the farm.

THE EARLY DAYS OF MARCH were always the axe-grinding days at Grandfather's. It was too cold to do much of anything yet too warm to do nothing at all. And so we ground the axes.

I CAN REMEMBER the excitement of watching the sparks fly from the hard steel as Grandfather placed a keen edge on all of the tools he would use in producing a good harvest. Grandfather ground his axe to perform a useful task because providing for his family was his life of Christian service.

HE GROUND HIS AXE to chop wood—not to chop people! We have all met people who have an axe to grind—who have pet peeves to prove—only they use us for the grindstone! They seem to relish the keen edge on their blade of idle gossip and contempt. They enjoy watching the sparks fly because they are our sparks and they light up what would have been a gloomy March morning.

PEOPLE who want to use us as grindstones always are around. They are even in the church. March seems to be axe-grinding time. Some are out looking for an axe to grind. They would like to be insulted so they can be insulting. During these gloomy days, when the sun does not always shine enough to dry up the mud, we Christians must exercise the extra mile of patience and good will.

WE MAY GRIND OUR AXE. But let us grind it on the grindstone that sharpens it for work—not on each other. Let us sharpen our minds and our tongues to speak of Christ—of the victory God has given us—not to slice the heart out of each other's service, so the Kingdom of God looks silly to the selfish seeker of salvation.

THESE ARE GLOOMY DAYS, but there is nothing gloomy about our salvation. I can remember one Spring day two years ago, when my parents and I took a little trip in the Allegheny Mountains of Northwestern Pennsylvania. We were traveling to Brady's Bend—a lookout point where you can see over twenty miles of river as it makes a huge horseshoe bend through the Allegheny Valley. I have never seen a finer view. But as we motored up the mountain on that gloomy day, a fog settled. At the lookout, we stumbled like blind people in the thick cloud, bumping every now and then against a monument or a signpost.

WE WERE ABOUT to give up and start the long journey home when a ray of sunshine burst through the heavy cloud. The fog began to lift. Soon, sunshine was bathing and transfiguring the mountain. The sunshine made me think of the Lord Jesus Christ. The world of his day, like the world today, was groping in a fog. We are not able to lift it ourselves. All of my might could not have dissipated the fog that blanketed Bray's Bend that morning. But what I could not do, the sun found to be an easy task. Where our human might unaided fails, the Light of the Child of God succeeds.

NOT OFTEN in the Bible do we read that "man is able," "woman is able." A hundred times we read, "God is able!" "Christ is able!" Cherish the confidence that some sweet day, the fogs of uncertainty, of doubt, of unbelief that are enveloping our lives right now will be in full retreat.

BEWARE the Ides of March. Look to the sunshine of the Cross of Jesus Christ.

AMEN.

THE KING RIDES IN MAJESTY

March 22, 1964
Palm Sunday
Trinity Lutheran Church, Galion, Ohio

TEXT: Romans 5: 6-8

FOR AT THE VERY TIME when we were still powerless, then Christ died for the wicked. Even for a just person, one of us would hardly die, though perhaps for a good person, one might actually brave death; but Christ died for us while we were yet sinners, and that is God's own proof of his love towards us.

WITH ATOMIC MISSILES poised over our heads, faith in God swept from under our feet, and the dust of materialism blinding our eyes—it is difficult for us to find a purpose or reason for living.

WE HAVE BECOME so engulfed in the sins of mankind that we hardly recognize sin when we see it today. A popular limerick lampoons the idea that sin really matters today:

There was a young girl from a mission,
Who was seized by a dreadful suspicion,
That original sin

Didn't matter a pin
In the era of nuclear fission.

TWO EXPRESSIONS from a recent issue of *Time* Magazine in
its review columns of books and movies give the characteristic
twentieth-century outlook on life: "The world is sick unto
death;" "Life is a dirty trick!"

WITH no promise for Tomorrow, we have lived for Today.
And we have "lived it up"—buying up pleasure, avoiding pain,
disavowing duty—forgetting God. "Eat, drink, and be merry, for
tomorrow we die!"

WHEN WILL DURANT, by questionnaire, asked the late
George Bernard Shaw, "What is the meaning of life?" the
English writer replied: "How the devil do I know?" To the same
question, H.L. Mencken answered: "I go on living for the same
reason a hen goes on laying eggs." Sounds futile, doesn't it?

DR. ROBERT A. MILLIKEN, a noted scientist of this century,
has well said: "Was it not two-thousand years ago in Galilee that
one lived of whom the whole thinking world still says—"Never
man spoke as this man?"

AND IT CAN BE RIGHTLY SAID: Never did a person live as
did Jesus Christ.

IN JESUS CHRIST, we see one who was born in an obscure
village, the child of a peasant woman. He grew up in another
obscure village. He worked in a carpenter shop until he was
thirty and then for three years he was an itinerant preacher. He
never wrote a book. He never held an office. He never had a
family. He never went to college. He never traveled two hundred
miles from the place he was born.

JESUS CHRIST NEVER DID one of the things that usually
accompanies greatness. He had no credentials but himself.
While he was yet a young man, the tide of popular opinion
turned against him. His friends ran away. One of them denied

him. He was turned over to his enemies. He went through the mockery of a Kangaroo Court. He was nailed on a cross between two thieves. His executioners gambled for the only piece of property he had on earth while he was dying—and that was his coat.

WHEN HE WAS DEAD, he was taken down and laid in a borrowed grave through the pity of a friend. The sceptic can only shake his head and ask: "And this was a king?"

NINETEEN CENTURIES have come and gone, and today the young man of Nazareth who "never quite made it" is still the centerpiece of the human race and the leader of a vast array of saints. Phillips Brooks has rightly said: "I am far within the mark when I say that all the armies that ever marched, and all the navies that were ever built, and all the parliaments that ever sat, and all the kings that ever reigned, put together, have not affected life of humans on earth as powerfully as that one solitary life."

LOOK AT US! We are sick unto death. We are helpless to save ourselves. Helpless to throw off the shackles of guilt, helpless to hold back the horror of the hydrogen bomb, helpless before the righteous judgment of God. We have followed the will-o'-the-wisp of worldly pleasure and promise only to find disenchantment and dull despair.

FOR PEOPLE like us, Christ rode into this world in majesty. For people like us, Christ died. At this very time when we are powerless to help ourselves, Christ has died for us. Christ died while we were yet sinners. Jesus could have been King but chose to wear the crown of thorns. That cross is God's proof of his love for us! That cross shows us the majesty of God!

INSTEAD of being a part of a "world sick unto death," through the cross we have the assurance of being alive for eternity. Life is no longer a dirty trick when through Christ it becomes love for eternity. Today we gather to celebrate the victory of the empty tomb!

"IT DOES NOT MATTER WHAT YOU BELIEVE, as long as you are sincere!" That is what they tell us so often today. But it does matter for us—if we are sincerely wrong.

HERE IS A TRAGIC STORY OF MISPLACED sincerity: Carbon dioxide was administered to a patient in a hospital in the state of New York, and death resulted instantly.

THE TRAGEDY occurred while the patient was being prepared for a minor operation. A trained anesthetist was administering a controlled mixture of oxygen and anesthetic gas when the tank of oxygen became exhausted. A new tank labeled "Oxygen" was substituted.

ALMOST IMMEDIATELY, the patient died. The attending surgeon and hospital authorities suspected some kind of accident and called the coroner. An autopsy revealed carbon dioxide poisoning. Upon examination, the "Oxygen" tank was found to contain carbon dioxide. The tank had been mislabeled before it reached the hospital.

THE MANUFACTURER was sincere. The hospital authorities were sincere. The anesthetist was sincere. The surgeon was sincere. And certainly, the patient was sincere. Not one of them wanted the tragedy to happen. They were all sincerely "wrong" about the oxygen—and instead of giving life, the poisoned air gave death.

SINCERITY is not enough. Certainty must be coupled with sincerity. Too many of us are saying too often: "As long as I am sincere, I'll come out all right in the end!"

BUT WE ARE SINCERELY MISTAKEN. Where our salvation is concerned, we must be certain—certain that we are obeying the will of God for us, certain that we are following the right Christ.

TOO MANY THINGS are mislabeled in our cellophane-wrapped modern world—"Forgiveness," "Life," "Peace," "Security," and "Salvation." The only way we can be absolutely certain in these matters is by taking our Lord at his word. No one is greater than God. No one is truer than God. Jesus said: "I am the Way, the Truth, and the Life: no one comes to the Creator, but by me!" And that took him to Jerusalem to die! And brings us today to celebrate the empty tomb!

THERE IS EVERY REASON in the world to take Jesus at his word and believe—for Jesus loved us to the point of dying for our sins on Calvary. Jesus rode in majesty on Palm Sunday, and Jesus kept on riding straight to Calvary. Jesus rode to victory in this life. Jesus now lives in the power of an endless life—and saves all who comes to God by Him! LIVE THAT!

THE FORGIVENESS OF THE CROSS

March 26, 1964
   Trinity Lutheran Church, Galion, Ohio
   Maundy Thursday, Holy Communion

ISAIAH 53: 4 & 5: Surely he hath borne our griefs, and carried our sorrows: yet we did esteem him stricken, smitten of God, and afflicted. But he was wounded for our transgressions, he was bruised for our iniquities: the chastisement of our peace was upon him and with his stripes we are healed.

WE COME to our Lord's table this evening to receive forgiveness for our sins and to gain assurance of our salvation.

A HINDU once asked a Christian missionary what he meant when he talked about salvation. After the missionary had given him a straightforward Biblical reply about God's forgiveness for our sins, the Hindu said, "That is exactly what I would have said!"

"OH," said the missionary. "What then is your assurance that your God is ready to forgive you?"

UNHESITANTLY HE REPLIED, "If he wouldn't, I would go to a God who did!"

THIS HINDU PROPHET tells us much about ourselves today. Far too often what we want personally becomes so important in our lives that God becomes secondary. We earnestly desire freedom from the trial of everyday living—to find a trail out of trouble, to receive the treasure of eternity.

YET for many of us, indeed, God has become secondary. If we cannot find salvation in front of the television set or at the movie theatre or at the bowling alley or at home in bed, then and only then do we turn to the cross of Jesus Christ and come to church. If any one of our "little gods" does not do the job, we turn to another, until hope runs out and we run to Christ!

COMPLETELY CONTRASTING this is the glorious Christian Gospel! The Bible tells us that the one living God of creation and judgment is the same God who at a particular place called Calvary revealed His saving grace on behalf of a world that did not care.

HE DIED to give us forgiveness. He died to set us free!

WE CAUSED CALVARY! It was the red-hot summer of our sin that forged the nails that tore through the flesh of his hands and feet. Our sins shocked through him with a searing pain with each beating blow of that heavy hammer. Our sins stooped his shoulder as he hung there and suffocated in silence on that black day. From the holes gouged in his hands and his feet dripped his life's blood—innocent blood that gives us forgiveness and hope.

Bearing shame and scoffing rude,
In my place condemned he stood;
Sealing my pardon with his blood,
Hallelujah! What a Savior!

IN THE DARKNESS of that hot afternoon, Jesus tasted death in all of its bitterness. In that dereliction, he paid the price of sin—my sins and your sins.

THEN HIS SPIRITUAL AGONY brought him physical

nausea. He uttered the cry, "I thirst"—the only cry of human suffering wrung from His lips. His swollen tongue and burning throat moistened by vinegar, Jesus summoned his fast-waning strength to exclaim triumphantly—finally and forever—"Finished! Finished!" Finished for you and for me—finally, forever. Jesus Christ walked to Calvary and won our freedom, so that we do not have to be forsaken!

TRAVELLER of life's highway, Jesus Christ took the road to the cross so we have forgiveness when we walk to His table tonight. Our God is ready to forgive us! Let us bring our bloody hands, our tired and weary hearts, our sin-sick souls to our Lord and Savior Jesus Christ. Thank God for the victory!

AMEN.

JESUS CHRIST IS RISEN TODAY

March 29, 1964
    Easter Morning
    Trinity Lutheran Church, Galion, Ohio

TEXT: 1 Corinthians 15: 16-19

FOR IF THE DEAD are not raised, it follows that Christ was not raised; and if Christ was not raised, your faith has nothing in it and you are still in your old state of sin. It follows also that those who have died within Christ's fellowship are utterly lost. If it is for this life only that Christ has given us hope, we of all people are most to be pitied.

IT WAS SUNDAY. A handful of men were hiding in a dark and dusty room, above a downtown shop. They were utterly miserable. They were discouraged, disheartened, and depressed. In their fear, that had bolted the door—not once but twice.

THE BOTTOM had fallen out of their world. All that they possessed had been given in loyalty to their leader. Everything had been centered in Him, and now—JESUS CHRIST WAS DEAD!

A CROSS—his cross—was silhouetted against the Eastern

sky in the early morning sunlight. A gruesome cross, a grim reminder of the death of all their hopes. His grave was in a garden close by. One more idealist removed from our world and with him all of his grand, but unfulfilled, promises.

TEAR-STREAKED FACES greeted the first rays of the early morning sun. Their eyes were dry now, but they were blotched red from rivers of weeping. After a while, tears would no longer come, but they were still crying inside. The world always weeps at the death of an idealist.

A FEW weeks later, these same men who shared that night-long wake together were on trial before those who were responsible for the death of their leader. The "crime" for which they were charged was that of preaching about him—telling others of what they had seen and heard. They were warned by their judges. They were beaten with heavy sticks until their backs were bruised—blue and bloody.

BUT THEY COULD NOT BE SILENCED! Brutal beatings could not quench their joy! The threat of death could not keep them quiet. What began as a rushing rumble on that Sunday morning as Peter and John ran back from the grave became a resonant roar! He has risen! Jesus Christ is alive!

I ONCE KNEW an old doctor who, like so many of his profession, was well-read and wise. He was a sincere and unashamed Christian. His scientific friends constantly tried to trap him into arguments concerning the miracles of the Bible and other religious problems.

MY FRIEND would reply: "Are you prepared to accept the fact of the Resurrection of Jesus Christ?" If they said "Yes," he could say, "Then there is no other problem you need trouble about!" If they said "No," he would say, "Then there is no use discussing anything else!"

IT WAS, perhaps, not a complete answer, but my old friend certainly put his finger on the fundamental issue of today and every other day—JESUS CHRIST IS RISEN FROM THE DEAD!!!

THE WHOLE TRUTH of our Christian faith stands or falls on the reality of the Resurrection. There are some who deny this. They say: "You die—then come back and tell me about it—and I'll believe!!"

OTHERS will not believe that Jesus Christ walked from his grave but will concede that the truth of his teaching and his spirit still walks in the church. But this will not do! The New Testament writers would have repudiated such an argument.

WHEN JESUS CHRIST was crucified, his closest friends earnestly believed it was all over—beautiful while it lasted, but ended just the same. Locked in their dreary little cells—away from prying eyes and pin-pricking gossip—they took little comfort in the fact of His life or the truth of His teaching.

IT WAS NOT until they had really grasped the fact that Christ had indeed risen from the dead that it all became true—so true that they were prepared to die to maintain it, and many of them did die to affirm it.

WRITING TO SOME PEOPLE who were trying to teach that Christ never rose, the Apostle Paul bluntly declared: "If Christ was not raised, your faith has nothing in it and you are still in your old state of sin. It follows also that most who have died within Christ's fellowship are utterly lost."

IN PLAIN WORDS, what Paul is telling us this morning is—if there be no resurrection, there is no Christian faith either for this life or for any other. We are, without the Resurrection of Jesus Christ, just playful puppets pulled by the blind forces of life. And when we die—we stay dead.

JESUS CHRIST HAS RISEN TODAY: ALLELUIA! The Resurrection message is one that can revolutionize our lives. Look what it did for the disciples. The clarion of Christ's Easter called them out of their self-made cells and changed them. The meek became magnetic servants at their Master's call, mustering all of their courage to march at Christ's command.

WHAT HAD HAPPENED? Why this change? They believed that their leader, Jesus Christ, was alive. They had seen him. They had spoken to him. Their enthusiasm stormed and finally won the Roman Empire. Their enthusiasm stormed and finally won you and me!

ALIVE FOR EVERMORE! That was the amazing message that captured the ancient world and has changed every breathing moment of our lives ever since.

AND WHERE IS OUR ENTHUSIASM this morning? Is it centered in the Resurrection of Jesus Christ? Or is it centered on the new dress or hat—in how pretty we look? Or is it centered on the boyfriend or girlfriend with whom we will spend most of today? Or is it centered in the basket of candy left at home—or on the bell that will end this service so we can get back to the business of baking hams, hunting for colored eggs in the park or our backyard?

THIRTY-SIX HOURS after Christ died on the cross, his grave was empty. Thirty-six hours after Good Friday 1964—will we leave this church with our hearts empty, our hopes empty, centering our lives in ourselves for another year instead of calling out the glad news that Jesus Christ is alive for evermore? Alive for you! Alive for me! Alive for eternity!

Death is destroyed. Evil is exterminated. Fear is forgotten. Jesus Christ is risen today! Our hope is alive! Our hearts are full!

WE PRAISE THEE, OH GOD, we acknowledge Thee to be the Lord.

UNTITLED

Our Debt is Paid; Our Credit is Good

April 5, 1964
    Trinity Lutheran Church, Galion, Ohio
    Quasimodo Geniti
    On the Occasion of the April Quarterly meeting.

TEXT: 1 Timothy 6: 17-19

INSTRUCT those who are rich in this world's goods not to be proud, and not to fix their hopes on so uncertain a thing as money, but upon God, who endows us richly with all things to enjoy. Tell them to hoard a wealth of noble actions by doing good, to be ready to give away and to share, and so acquire a treasure which will form a good foundation for the future. Thus, they will grasp the life which is life indeed.

SUPPOSE you are one thousand dollars in debt to the largest department store in this city, or any other city. You have no money to pay, and have no credit to borrow any money. The store keeps sending you bills, and you keep hoping that you will find a way to pay, but you do not.

THEY THREATEN TO SUE, but you still cannot pay. You get another letter from the store. You say to yourself: "Another bill! What shall I do? Perhaps I'll have to go to jail this time!"

AND YOU OPEN THE LETTER fretfully, forlornly—full of frustration and fear. You read: "Dear Customer: We are glad to notify you that a friend of yours who does not wish to have his name known, has come in and paid your bill in full. More than that, he has deposited another thousand dollars to your credit. Now—instead of you owing us one thousand dollars—we owe you one thousand dollars. Please come in and use your credit."

YOU ARE AMAZED—of course you are! You can say one of three things:

"THAT MUST be a mistake! I have no friend who thinks that much of me. Tomorrow I will go down to that store and tell them they have their accounts confused." That would be unbelief.

OR YOU COULD SAY: "I appreciate that friend's desire to help, but I cannot allow it. I am what I am! I make my own way in this world. No one is going to pay my bills but me." That would be rejection.

OR YOU MAY SAY: "Thank God for such a friend! Come on, wife, let's go down to the store and use our credit!" That would be faith.

BY DYING on the cross, Jesus Christ has paid the entire debt to God for our sins. His Easter victory has wiped the slate clean in remission for our sins. But it has done even more than that for each one of us. It has put all of the righteousness of Christ down to our credit. We are not only out of debt, but we have as much credit standing as Jesus Christ can give us. Our security is everlasting life—a life beautiful and bountiful—a life that never ends.

WE CAN BE unbelieving, rejecting, or accepting. Ours is the choice.

"IMPOSSIBLE," say some. "Trinity Church has remained the same size for a score of years! She will never grow!" This is unbelief. Anywhere during the long history of the Christian church where the Spirit of God has been permitted to work freely—the Christian church has grown. Anywhere a band of Christians has looked beyond themselves, they have found success. Consider the day of Pentecost—three thousand people brought into the church by a handful that numbered twelve. How much more could God's Spirit accomplish here today working through two-hundred consecrated men and women—if only we would let Jesus Christ in—let Him work here—take His word at its faith value, instead of looking only at the face value of everything new and untried.

GOD'S SPIRIT already is at work here. We can see it in our choir, in our young people, in the women of the church, in the crowded church school, in all of the willing hands and prayerful hearts that have accomplished so much during these past months.

MANY think it folly to try to do again what our father did here so many years ago. But the growth of the Christian church has appeared foolish for centuries. The Pharisees laughed at Jesus, then at Peter and at Paul. The Pope in Rome said that Luther ought to be in Bedlam. The men of his own church thought Xavier was mad. All England laughed at John Wesley. Many people think that Billy Graham is not quite sane. Laughter like this has run through the centuries, but it has not stopped the growth of the Christian church.

WE ARE NOT HELPLESS—just as our father who placed those beams and carried these bricks were not helpless. We have a head start on the first Christian church. There was a helpless church—without teachers, without a written Bible, without past experience, without knowledge. No wonder Paul was concerned about their continuance in the faith. No wonder he prayed for them constantly, continually, without ceasing. But they believed —and they built. Today we believe! We must build too!

"IMPOSSIBLE?" Not here at Trinity Church. Our pews are bulging. The back of this proud old building is breaking. We must build for the glory of God.

MANY STILL SAY: "I appreciate the zeal to follow God's Spirit and build—but we cannot allow it. We cannot afford to go the whole way—tomorrow maybe, but not today." This is rejection. If our dedicated pastors and fathers yesterday had waited for tomorrow, there would be no today! Trinity would have passed away when they passed away. This beautiful building would not be here today.

IT WAS A STRUGGLE for them to erect this building during the Depression. The good pastor and people of this congregation agonized through many a long and lonely night to produce for you and for me the most beautiful and the most perfect church building in this town. Our fathers had little but faith, but they gave the best of all they had to God. They built God's house out of finer stuff than their own homes. And they lived like kings and queens on day-old bread to pay for it—and gave God all the glory.

IT WAS A STRUGGLE—yes—but it was a struggle that made them strong.

THERE IS THE STORY about two brothers who were mountain climbers. I can get excited about mountain climbing —for is that not what we all want to do? Climb a mountain of one kind or another? The two brothers met an accident one wintry afternoon as they were climbing across an icy cliff. Caught by a sudden avalanche of snow, they were tossed like a feather's weight down the mountainside. The one brother disappeared under the falling snow. The other was thrown clear where he lay dazed for perhaps minutes or an hour—he could not remember.

WHEN HE CAME TO, his head was pounding furiously. His hands were shaking from shock. He was so cold he could not feel his feet. But forgetting himself the love of his brother, he began to call out: "Hans, Hans, where are you???"

REMEMBERING the avalanche, he began to dig in the snow with his fingers with all the fury of a madman, compelled by his mission. As he labored, the sun set. It was dusk when he uncovered a snowy boot, a leg, and then his brother's body—all still and blue.

THERE WAS A FAINT HEARTBEAT—Hans was still alive. With his remaining energy, he dragged his brother behind a fallen log, away from the biting wind. Taking off his own coat, he covered him up. For added warmth, he lay on top of him, and he forced breath into his brother's lungs.

IT WAS NOT until Hans had opened his eyes and attempted a weak smile that the brother noticed that he was warm all over —in fact, he had broken out in a sweat. His hands and his bare arms were red. He could feel his feet again! His struggle to save his brother's life made him strong—and probably saved his own life, too!

IT IS TRUE! To struggle often makes us strong. If we walk the easy way all of our Christian lives, we will become spiritual weaklings. Jesus Christ struggled on Calvary and won for us the victory. He was no spiritual weakling. Our fathers struggled to build this church, and their faith made them strong. They were not spiritual weaklings.

DARE we choose for ourselves a road for the next decade that will not be a struggle? What will happen to the faith of our fathers, if we do not have the faith of our fathers?

WE MUST FORGET ourselves at the call of Christ. To build up this church and serve our community here at His command will not be easy. Christ never told us that his life would be easy. All He tells us is that His life is the best—the best that there is.

He gave His best for us to stamp Paid in Full cross the awful debt of our sin. Can we give any less than our best back to Him at His call?

TO BUILD a new church here will mean struggle and sacrifice, for we are not many and we do not have much, but it will make us strong. We will shine like saints for all of Galion to see. We will be secure for eternity.

ON THE CROSS, our debt has been paid. Our credit is Christ, and it is good. Let us build—as believers, as men and women of faith—and let this proud old church grow to the glory of God!

AMEN.

HELP US, LORD!

April 19, 1964
Trinity Lutheran Church, Galion, Ohio
Jubilate: 3rd Sunday After Easter

TEXT: 1 Thessalonians 5:17
PRAY without ceasing.

"HELP ME, LORD!" This human cry is prayer. A schoolboy has struggled for hours with an algebra problem that he cannot solve. Finally, he prays, "Help me, Lord!"

A YOUNG MAN is in a foxhole in a strange land. Frightening flashes light up even a stranger night sky. Smoke stings his eyes and fine bits of steel toss the dirt around him into an angry cloud of dust. A whistle blows. The attack begins. That instant, the soldier is all alone. Will he be brave or a coward? Will he have courage to go forward? "Help me, Lord!"

THIS YOUNG GIRL is confronted with a hard decision. On one hand is wealth and prestige—that is, if she lowers the flag of her ideal just a little. "Everybody else is doing it—you will too if you want to be popular!" her friends tell her. In spite of the pressure of her peers, she keeps her self-respect, keeps faith with her

Christian heritage, keeps faith with Christ herself. She cries out: "Help me, Lord!"

A YOUNG MOTHER—her lover ran out and left her with the kids and all the bills—comes to the end of her rope. She kneels and prays: "Help me, Lord!"

I KNOW of another young man who is engrossed in his work. It is a work of service to his fellows. He is very busy. During his working hours that often go far into the night, he has not much time to think about religion. But he never fails to stop by his church at the beginning of each day to ask the prayer, "Help me, Lord!

IT IS A HUMAN CRY! It is a cry to God. It is prayer.

WHEN WE CRY out of the bottom of the pitch-black pit of our frustration and fear—"HELP ME, LORD!"—we recognize that God is God, that God is compassionate, that God hears, that God is loving and willing to help. Uttering this simple prayer, we cut the ribbon that opens up a wide freeway through which God's blessing may flow into our lives.

DOES GOD answer our prayer? Yes, God helps! Why else would we pray? Of course, we are not thinking of the petty prayers of conscience, which are not prayers at all.

NO DOUBT you have heard of the little girl who was asked in school, "What is the capital of Ohio?" On her paper, she wrote in big, bold letters: "KENTUCKY!" That night at home, she discovered her mistake and she turned to God for help, "O God," she prayed, "please make Kentucky the capital of Ohio—Try to have it done by 9:00 tomorrow morning."

TOO OFTEN we have become burdened by little things that allow our praying to become petty and self-pleasing, laboring under the assumption that if our prayers please us, they will also please God. Far too often, we underestimate the value of prayer in our lives and in our church. Prayer is powerful. That is God's promise.

GOD HAS MADE another promise, too. Jesus told us: "Where two or three are gathered in my name—there am I." Too long we have neglected the power of God's kind of prayer—where Christians gather together into small groups not to pour coffee, but to pray without ceasing.

"HELP ME, LORD!" can become "Help us, Lord!" when two or three are gathered together—all aware of the same problems and needs, all facing the same decision. There is Christ! There is power! There is peace and happiness. This kind of prayer takes perspiration, but it knows power and it pleases God. "Help us, Lord!" is the prayer of dedicated Christians, who know and feel that together they are each one bound up in the bundle of humanity and responsible for the needs of everyone.

"WHY DO WE fight so much at church?" a concerned Christian asked this pastor last week. Perhaps we would not fight so much if we would pray a little more. If we would come to the realization that we are responsible for each other, perhaps, we would learn to love each other more.

A RADIO BROADCASTER made this unforgettable statement: "Sometimes I get to broadcasting when I ought to be tuning in!" Do we not all do this too often where prayer is concerned—broadcast when we ought to be tuning in? At church we allow the book to pray for us. At home, our memorized prayers bounce off the walls and rattle through the air while our minds wander around more exciting things.

THEN we complain bitter about the spiritual ignorance of children today. For example, a confirmation class was asked, "What is Prayer?" One eighth grader wrote: "Prayer is what preachers open and close meetings with." To the question, "Do You Pray?, another wrote: "I don't know!"

AND WE COMPLAIN about all of the pain and pressure of our "quick frozen, pop it into the oven until it's golden brown" age. But when the call comes, "Come over and pray with me!"

we answer with all of the spiritual energy of St Paul: "I'm too busy today, or this week—contact me in the fall!" Or—"I appreciate your asking, but I do all of my praying at home!"

IF WE ARE willing to meet together to bowl, to throw darts, to sew, and to talk over a cup of coffee, we ought to be more than willing to meet together to talk to God.

A TREE must not only have a trunk and branches. If it is going to survive and grow, it must have a root system that compares in size to the trunk and branches. The Christian Church cannot survive and grow by just having a new building and more people. We must have roots that cling to Christ. And these roots feed on a sea of prayer.

IT TAKES PEOPLE—you and me people—praying together, pouring out our hearts together, preserving here the power of God to give us strength to survive the struggle that lies ahead.

TRINITY has a prayer group. Will you make the sacrifice to come, and learn, and pray?

I do not undertake to say
That literal answers come from heaven,
But this I know—that when I pray
A comfort, a support is given
That helps me soar over earthly things,
As a robin flies up on airy wings.

Prayer is a sweet, refining grace
That educates the soul and heart;
It lends a luster to the face,
And by its elevating art
It gives the mind an inner sight
That makes all of life come out all right.

From our little selves it helps us rise
To something "Godly" that we may yet be!

And so, I do not ask to be wise,
If thus my faith is lost to me,
Faith that with angelic voice and touch,
Says: "Pray, for prayer availeth much!"

AMEN.

NOT WITHOUT WARNING

May 3, 1964
    Trinity Lutheran Church, Galion, Ohio
    Rogate: Fourth Sunday After Easter

TEXT: 1 John 1:8-10
    IF WE SAY we have no sin, we deceive ourselves, and the
truth is not in us. If we confess our sins, he is faithful and just,
and will forgive our sins and cleanse us from all unrighteous-
ness. If we say we have not sinned, we make God a liar, and
God's word is not in us.
    THERE IT STOOD, proud in its exotic beauty, the show-
piece of northeastern Italy. The massive Vajont Dam, only three
years old, linked the rocky cliffs of a spectacular gorge. Behind it,
the deep blue of lake and mountains shimmered in the glow of
the star-filled night.
    CLOSE BELOW THE DAM, the little village of Longarone
was quiet except for the bursting from village windows of the
TV announcer's breathless description of a championship
soccer match.
    IT WAS 10:43, October 9, 1963. An explosive roar thundered

along the valley, rousing some from their TV sets. A sudden
storm, they thought. The scream of the wind shook the rooftops.
They closed the green and blue shutters and turned back to the
soccer match. Moments later, a valley drowned!

IT HAD NOT BEEN THE SCREAM of the wind. Instead, a
mountain had fallen into the reservoir above the dam, spilling
the lake into a giant curved wave of doom that splashed first
against the cliffs and then hurled its flood into the gorge below.

DEATH WITHOUT WARNING! The story repeats itself
almost daily. We no longer need to recount the fate of Pompeii
for an illustration of sudden death. We see it all about us. There
is the squealing of overheated brakes—the smell of burning
rubber—the heavy thud of collision. Broken bones. Blood on
the street. Death without warning!

There was the little Iranian village of Ghazel Gashlag, where
the village chief sipped his tea and settled on his mat for the
night, never to move from that spot. He was one of 10,000 who
perished at exactly 10:52 on the night of September 1, 1962, when
a great earthquake shattered nearly 400 towns and villages.

THERE WAS Hurricane Flora. The earthquake in Alaska—
endless death and destruction!

THERE WAS THAT LITTLE SWISS VILLAGE that sent a
fourth of its population on that first exciting airplane trip into
the skies—only to bury someone from every home before many
hours had passed.

THERE WAS the submarine Thresher that pointed its nose
deep into the sea on April 10, 1963—never to return. There was
the sudden storm last week in Northern Ohio—

DEATH WITHOUT WARNING!

DID ALL of these thousands of people have the opportunity
that we have this morning to repent and be forgiven? Was there
no voice of mercy calling in that last hour to Pompeii—Alaska—

and Longarone? Or did the voice of the Spirit of God speak most loudly just before it was forever silenced?

A NUMBER of years ago, a man named Luther Warren, a mighty power in the pulpit, was invited to give a series of lectures in Jamaica. A large hall was rented in the city of Kingston, and young ministers for miles around were invited in to watch this man in action.

ON THE FIRST NIGHT, the hall was crowded. The young ministers were there in the front seats. Luther Warren stepped to the desk.

BUT SOMETHING STRANGE happened. In a few minutes, he had covered his announced subject and turned to another. Then another. He had left introductory truth behind and had turned to the most vital issues that claim our attention in our last hour. He talked of obedience. He talked of judgment. He talked of forgiveness. He talked of decision. As those who had sponsored him watched in amazement from the rear of the auditorium, he invited men and women to step to the altar in complete commitment. And the people surged forward under the power of deep conviction.

WHY HAD HE PREACHED as he did? Why had he touched every challenging truth in one night? No one knew. Luther Warren himself did not know.

BUT THE NEXT MORNING, they all knew. For a large part of Kingston lay in ruins at the hand of a great earthquake. There had been only one night.

I ASK YOU, isn't it like our God to send a last warning message? Can you imagine a world-destroying flood without a Noah? Can you imagine the great apostasy of Elijah's day without the prophet's decisive voice? Can you imagine Christ's invading human history as He did without John's preparing the way?

CAN YOU IMAGINE dying, without knowing that you are forgiven?

AWOMAN ONCE CONFIDED in me at a funeral of how happy she was that God had spared her sister long enough for her to come hundreds of miles to ask her forgiveness. They had had a squabble as young girls and had not spoken or written for years. "I never would have forgiven myself," she said, "if I could not have told Betty how sorry I am before she died!"

WE LIVE our lives as if death will never come—as if death without warning is impossible. Perhaps this is why sisters and brothers fuss and fight with each other. Perhaps this is why sons and daughters wait until next week to visit their lonely mother or father who is only a few miles away. Perhaps if we would say the words "I FORGIVE YOU!"—we would not have anything to grumble or complain about!

"I FORGIVE YOU!" Those words demand that we look at ourselves. True forgiveness demands proof. True forgiveness demands that we change our way of thinking and of living. True forgiveness may even demand our life.

JESUS CHRIST FORGIVES US. He proved it by dying for us. On the cross he cried out of his agony: "Father, forgive them. They know not what they do!" We do not know what tomorrow will bring—whether we will live or we will die. But we do know that when we step up to the Lord's Table this morning, WE ARE FORGIVEN. No matter what we have done, the slate has been wiped clean, the broken record has been mended, our heavenly home is secure again—WE ARE ONE WITH OUR LORD IN HIS BODY AND BLOOD!

Jesus Christ has forgiven us! Dare we not forgive each other—before one more hour passes on this earth?

AMEN.

WE LOVE YOU, MOTHER!

May 10, 1964
Trinity Lutheran Church, Galion, Ohio
Fifth Sunday After Easter

Mother's Day 1964

TEXT: Proverbs 31:30.
"Charm is deceitful, and beauty is vain, but a woman who fears the Lord is to be praised."

A LAD made his way to the lingerie section of a big department store to buy a Mother's Day gift. "I want to buy my mom a slip," he told the clerk. But when it came to giving the information as to size, he was at something of a loss.

"IT WOULD HELP," the clerk suggested, "if you could tell me whether your mother is tall or short, fat or slim."

"OH," said the boy, "She's just perfect!"

So, the clerk wrapped up a size 34 for him and on the next day, Mom herself was in to exchange it for a size 52!

MOTHER! SHE'S JUST PERFECT! Few of us remember much if anything of what our mothers looked like when they were in the full bloom of their youth—but for us today, she is just perfect. Is there anyone who ever thought his mother was ugly? She is just right for us—she's just perfect. She has been God's gift to us.

IT IS DIFFICULT in our weary world for a mother to be perfect—and still wash all the diapers, mow the lawn, do the shopping, sew, scrub, cook, and look her Sunday best when Father comes home to dinner. But Christ calls mothers of today to be perfect—to meet the challenge of the glad Christian gospel and to carry it on to their children.

THE UNIVERSAL PLEA of every woman as she gives birth to her first child is the most beautiful prayer I have ever heard. Out of all the pain and misery at the mystery of birth, the Christian mother calls out to her God: "O Lord, make him prefect and make life better for him than it has been for me!"

IS THAT NOT JUST LIKE a mother, to want to make things just a little bit better for each one of us? Somehow, mothers do not get much credit for doing Christ's work in the home. Usually, the thankless task of disciplining the children falls on her—and she is known as the "mean one" of the family.

WHILE FATHER is at work during the day, it is Mother who is there all of the time. She is commonplace. So, it is a treat when Dad comes home. My wife tells of how she and her sister, Louise, would spend the last ten minutes or so before their father was expected home looking for his car through the panes of the front window. Periodically, they would call out: "Daddy! Daddy, please come home!"

At our home, when we went shopping, our parents used to split us up between them. One went with Dad, one with Mother. It was always a fight over who got to go with Dad. Neither one of us wanted to go with Mother. We spent every day with her.

YET, when we were sick or frightened or hurt, where did we always run? There was no place better to wipe away tears than on Mother's apron. It never seemed to burn as long when mother put on the iodine. Her hands were always the softest. She always knew the right place to scratch.

OUR FIRST PRAYERS did not seem like they would reach all the way up to heaven—and God—unless Mother knelt by the bed and heard them said.

MOTHERS HAVE a lasting influence on their children. Even today, I am uneasy during a thunderstorm because I was frightened as a child by seeing my mother run to the chicken house in the midst of a storm, with lightning striking all around her—fearing that she would never come back to where I stood crying by the window.

THIS IS WHY I think it is important enough in the Christian Church to set aside one day to talk about mothers.

THERE ARE TOO MANY mothers and fathers in our world who are not Christian. Even though they may belong to a church, they are not Christian, because they do not teach Christ in the home. And when their children grow up, they mumble and complain that they are ungrateful—that they don't love them, or don't care, or don't have any moral or spiritual values.

AND YET how many times I have seen mothers walk down the streets of our town with one baby, who cannot yet walk, in a stroller, and another on her arm—a cigarette in her lips, blowing smoke in the child's face as she admonishes him for crying because he is hungry and such a nuisance.

WE EXPECT OUR CHILDREN to grow up and speak like men and women, but instead of teaching them the gospel as we promised to do, we talk to them in baby talk. "If you don't walk the chalk line, the Boogey Man is going to get you before you grow up!" Before we know it, they do grow up—and to grab, to hoard, to curse and shout becomes their way of life, too!

BUT FOR THOSE of us who have been blessed with Christian mothers, this has not been the case. We have happy memories of all the very infrequent occasions when she had time to talk and play with us. Sitting at the little maple table and chairs, she taught us how to use modeling clay. I can still see the little brown bird's nest she made one day—with the blue clay balls for eggs—and she told us how God loves and cares for the birds in the trees, just as he cares for us. I thought that surely no one in the world could have made anything so perfect.

AND HAVE YOU EVER smelled anything so good as home-baked bread? There was always a warm heel of bread, loaded with melting butter. One for Dad and Sister—and two for me!

MOTHER did not get any of this "best" part of the bread, but she would smile with satisfaction while we thanked God and ate and dropped crumbs onto the floor. She was not just baking bread. She was building a home.

A house is built of bricks and stones
Of sills, of posts and piers,
But a home is built of loving deeds
That stand a thousand years.

A house, though rough and humble,
    Within its walls may hold
A home of priceless beauty,
    Rich in love's eternal gold.

The men of earth build houses, sills
    And chambers, roofs and domes.
But the women of the earth,
    God knows, the women make the homes.

AND SO, I thank God this morning for the mothers of Trinity Church! For the beauty of your detergent-reddened hands. For your brows wrinkled because you care. For all the tears that you have shed in silent hurt, because your children bicker and fight, and fail to meet the challenge you have given them. For the silent prayers that you have called up to heaven at a baby's cough, a young man's cry of pain, at a husband's misunderstanding.

WE LOVE YOU, MOTHER, not only for what you are, but for what you are when we are with you. We love you, not only for what you have made of yourself, but for what you are making of us.

WE LOVE YOU, MOTHER, for putting your hand into our heaped-up hearts and passing over all the foolish, weak things that you cannot help seeing there, and for drawing out into the light all the beautiful belongings that no one else, except God himself, has looked quite far enough to find.

GOD LOVES YOU, MOTHER! For you are helping to make out of the lumber of our lives—not a tavern, but a temple—not sin, but a song.

AND YOU HAVE DONE IT without a touch, without a word, without a sign. You have done it by being yourself.

AMEN.

KEEP THE FACE OF JESUS BEFORE YOU

May 17, 1964
   Trinity Lutheran Church, Galion, Ohio
   Pentecost Day

Message to My First confirmation Class

TEXT: Hebrews 3: 12-14
   SEE TO IT, brothers, that no one among you has the wicked, faithless heart of a deserter from the living God. But day by day, while that word "today" still sounds in your ears, encourage one another, so that no one of you is made stubborn by the wiles of sin. For we have become Christ's partners if only we keep our original confidence firm to the end.
   THIS IS FOR our confirmation class. It is a short message written especially for them, but it might mean something for you too.
   "JIMMY," said the pastor, "have you prayed to God today?"
   The young pastor was visiting a little boy in Children's Hospital. The small room was dim and light green—and it

smelled of medicine. The boy was too big for the bed on which he was lying. His feet stuck through the iron bars at the bottom end. He was seriously ill and in great pain.

"BUT I DON'T KNOW GOD!" said the little sufferer.

THERE WAS A PAUSE. Then his face lighted up and he said, "But I do know Jesus. I learned in Sunday School that he liked little children, and I read stories of how he laid hands on the sick and healed them."

"THAT'S ALL you need to know, Jimmy!" said the Pastor. "When you are talking to God, keep the face of Jesus before you."

"I LIKE THE JESUS GOD," MURMERED the little fellow, as he turned his head on his pillow and fell asleep.

YOU WILL GROW only one day older today, but as you leave this church, you will stand much taller, for you will have said YES to the call of Jesus Christ and have become a member of His Church and affirmed that membership by Holy Communion.

THE MESSAGE that I bring to you this morning before you step up to be confirmed is the same message that I brought to Jimmy. As you step forward onto the rough and rutted road of your Christian life—KEEP THE FACE OF JESUS BEFORE YOU.

YOU DO NOT know much about God, even though you have studied His word for three years in confirmation school. God is too big for that! But you do know Jesus! And that makes the difference. That is what brings you here today.

THE PROMISES you affirm today will become more important to you as you grow older and more mature in your Christian faith. This day with all of its excitement probably means more to your parents than it does for you. They have counted their blessings as they watched you grow up and blossom according to

God's plan. You have brought happiness to your parents as young children, and you will bring them great joy as young adults.

TODAY probably means more to you as an end. It's all over! Those endless Saturday mornings spent at church, yawning, watching the weary hour wander on the basement clock. It seemed to be the slowest clock in the world, didn't it?

AND TODAY may mean little more than the end of those Saturday mornings and the fretful Friday evenings spent studying or being told to study. And for some strange reason, the meanings repeated perfectly to yourself as you fell asleep never seemed to come out so easily in front of the pastor the next day.

CONFIRMATION may mean little more than new clothes, a few gifts, visits from the relatives, and—perhaps—a party.

IT'S ALL OVER! But confirmation is not an end. It is the beginning of your active Christian life. With confirmation, you will enjoy all of the privileges of the Christian Church—but you also must begin to carry with you today your share of the responsibility for Christ's Church.

DURING the next few years, the world will make many demands on your time. As you all move over to the high school, you will become involved in so many activities that you will be tempted to place the Church last.

"I DON'T HAVE TIME!" You may say—or more honestly —"I don't want to!"

I AM REMINDED of a sign that hangs on the wall behind the desk of the Dean of Men of Capital University. In tall letters, framed in black, are the words: "I'M THIRD!"

WHEN asked what this means, John Kirker points to the sign in his busy office and says, "Jesus Christ is first in my life. The Church is second. I'm third!"

MAKE THIS DAY a real beginning. Make yourself a real

blessing for Trinity Church, for Trinity Church has already been a blessing for you in many ways. If you keep the face of Jesus before you—He will always be first—and you will be second to none.

AMEN.

CHANGING THE GEARS OF OUR LIVES

May 24, 1964
   Trinity Lutheran Church, Galion, Ohio
   Trinity Sunday

After an article by Stanley Harris

TEXT: Galatians 3:1
   "O FOOLISH GALATIANS, who has bewitched you?"
   ONE DAY a young man came to William E. Gladstone, a great English statesman and an outstanding Christian. "Mr. Gladstone, I would appreciate your giving me a few minutes in which I could lay before you the plans for my future. I would like to study the law!"
   "YES," said the great statesman, "and what then?"
   "THEN, SIR, I hope to pass my examination to the bar."
   "YES, YOUNG MAN, AND WHAT THEN?"
   "THEN, SIR, I hope to have a place in Parliament, in the house of Lords."
   "YES, YOUNG MAN, AND WHAT THEN?" asked Gladstone.

"THEN I hope to do great things for my country."

"YES, YOUNG MAN, AND WHAT THEN?"

"THEN, SIR, I hope to retire and take life easy."

"YES, YOUNG MAN, and what then?" Gladstone tenaciously asked.

"WELL, THEN, MR. GLADSTONE, I suppose I will die."

"YES, YOUNG MAN, AND WHAT THEN?"

THE YOUNG MAN hesitated and said, "I never thought any further than that, sir!"

STERNLY and steadily, Gladstone stared at the young man and said: "Young man, you are a fool! Go home and think life through!"

THERE ARE a great many of us in the world just like that young man, making a multitude of plans every day that we live without taking God into consideration. We are just like the young ruler who came to Jesus asking about eternal life. He was held in high honor. He lived a life of ease. He was prominent in the social life of his community. But, as Christ pointed out, he was destitute of the Christian graces. He did not want to sacrifice his power and wealth, even though eternal life was at stake.

NEVER in the history of mankind have so many people been blessed with so much, particularly in America. But the material things that we enjoy every day are not the ultimate answer to our spiritual needs. Our most pressing need is to find God and His way of life.

PETER MARSHALL, the beloved former chaplain of the United States Senate, prayed, "Our Father, we are beginning to understand at last that the things that are wrong with our world are the sum total of all the things that are wrong with us as individuals. Most of us know perfectly well what we ought to do. Our trouble is that we do not want to do it. Thy help is our only hope. Make us to want to do what is right, and give us the ability to do it. Reach down and change the gears within us that we may go forward with Thee. Amen."

OUR WORLD is moving forward rapidly and without reason. We are constantly discovering the better mousetrap, the tar-less cigarette, and the perfect deodorant. We appear to be bewitched by a brazen and unfeeling way of life that gets bigger and better every day. The question asked by Paul so many centuries ago seems to fit us today: "Who has bewitched you?" We have bewitched ourselves. We need, as Peter Marshall has said, to have God "reach down and change the gears within us."

TODAY the cry is for wine, women, and song as our world indulges in all of the colored lights and gaiety of a mad carnival of death. Divorce increases. Crime is rising up like a Frankenstein monster. Juvenile problems—especially alcoholism—are at their highest in Franklin County. Immorality, disease, and suicide are increasing in a frightening manner. The love of position, possessions, and ease—the three deadly sins of modern life —is the distemper, the downfall, the damnation of our world.

RUSSELL LYNES, author of *A Surfeit of Honey*, says, "What is so all-fired wonderful about our prosperity? People are getting ruder. Service of all kinds is deteriorating. Juveniles are getting more delinquent. Traffic is becoming impossible."

WE ARE BUILDING bigger and better houses, churches, hospitals, cars, and appliances. We are planting more flower gardens and organizing bigger and better school districts for our children. We are a great swarming ant heap of a country with riches and plenty.

WE HAVE EVERYTHING—except security and happiness —AND GOD! We want certainty. We want comfort. But we have found little but the aspirin bottle and black despair.

ONE DAY, a teacher in a Christian school asked her students if they were planning to go to heaven. They all raised their hands except one boy. When the teacher asked him why he had no desire to go to heaven, he answered, "Mother and Sis want to go, but I'm going with Dad!"

THE TEACHER LATER talked with the father, a prominent physician. When told what had happened, he broke down and confessed that he had not been a good example for his son. He admitted that he spent every hour of his working week in gaining wealth and position. Sunday was his day off. He usually went fishing and took his son with him. His life revealed a lack of interest in eternal things, and his boy had followed him.

TODAY IS TRINITY SUNDAY. We are not in any danger from war here at home. Dinner is waiting for us at home. Our houses are relatively secure when we lock them up at night. But eternity? Is eternity just as secure for each one of us today? When we opened our worship this morning in the Name of the Father, and of the Son, and of the Holy Ghost—we stated everything that we know about God.

THE BIBLE teaches that God is actually three persons. This is a mystery that we will never be able to fully understand. The Bible does not teach that there are three Gods—but there is one God. This one God, however, is expressed in three persons. There is God the Father, God the Son, and God the Spirit.

THE SEOND PERSON of this Trinity is God's Son, Jesus Christ. He is co-equal with God the Father. He is not a Son of God, but *the* Son of God. He is the eternal Son of God—the second person of the Holy Trinity, God in the flesh, the living Savior.

GOD'S SPIRIT lives inside of those who sincerely desire to follow His way. Our world is a training school for the future home of the redeemed. We never fully know what God is getting us ready for. One time a preacher prayed: "Father, prepare us for what Thou art preparing for us!"

WHEN ELISHA followed the plow, he did not know what God had in store for him. Moses at the burning bush did not

Changing the Gears of Our Lives   207

know. When God called Paul on the Damascus Road, he did not know. But we, who are caught up in the "rat race" of this life with all of its temptations and frustrations, do know what God has planned for us. His plan is that one day at his call, we will come to be with him. Because Christ died for us, we are able to plan beyond our earthly lifetime—for in Him we see our salvation for eternity.

THERE WAS A WELL-KNOWN man who had spent his life in the accumulation of wealth and power. Along the way, he had also accumulated many sinful habits. He lived out his later years friendless and in wretched misery. When he was asked, "If you could see God face to face and talk to Him, what would you ask Him to do for you?"

HE ANSWERED QUICKLY: "I would have Him make me over again!"

THIS is exactly what our Savior proposes to do for everyone who asks. If we allow Him, He will reach down and change the gears of our lives. Just as we are world-centered, we can become God-centered.

SAD TO SAY, there are some women who would rather have a mink coat than the robe of righteousness. Some men would rather have great wealth than a Christian character. But to those of us who truly want peace, and hope, and eternal salvation—God promises to make life over again—to prepare us for what He is preparing for us.

JUST ONE chance have we at the earthly life. It will soon be gone.

AMEN.

WILL THIS CHURCH LIVE OR DIE?

May 31, 1964
   Trinity Lutheran Church, Galion, Ohio
   Trinity I

TEXT: Psalm 51: 3-4
   FOR I KNOW my transgressions, and my sin is ever before me. Against thee, thee only, have I sinned, and done that which is evil in thy sight, so that thou art justified in thy sentence and blameless in thy judgment.
   ONLY ONCE in my short lifetime have I seen an entire Christian congregation cry. It happened one Sunday morning while I was worshiping at First English Lutheran Church in Columbus. It was some ten years ago when Dr. Harold Albert was pastor.
   AFTER the Gospel lesson, Pastor Albert paused briefly and then took a water-soaked letter out of his hymnal. It was the familiar handwriting of a Lutheran missionary. He began to read slowly.
   "DEAR CHRISTIAN PEOPLE: I am writing this to you twelve thousand feet in the air as my plane takes me back to my

work in India. Thank you for sending the $700 you have
promised for an X-ray machine in our clinic. I have faith in God
that the money you promised for an X-ray machine will be there
when the plane lands. Thank you and God bless you wonderful
people."

THE ADDITIONAL WRITING was illegible and scorched.
Pastor Albert solemnly explained how the plane had crashed,
the missionary had died, and the letter was all that was left.

PLACING the fragment back into his hymnal, Pastor Albert
said to his people: "In good faith, we promised to give $700. On
faith, our departed brother has thanked us in his death, for a
sum of money that would not have been in India had he lived to
land. We promised $700, but when it became time to give and
the plate passed each one of us...we gave only $64.50.

A BOY in front of me burst into tears. Some wept openly.
Others coughed and reached for handkerchiefs. It was sponta-
neous! A whole people of God weeping, weeping because they
had failed to live up to their promise to God.

I AM SAD TODAY. I am weeping, because of the state of
things in our church. On faith last April 5th, we made a promise.
We have committed ourselves to the task of building a church.
We have said that we would do it, but for the most part, we are
just sitting and smoldering, secure in our sin.

THIS IS AN OLD STORY: You have heard it before. Dedicated pastors have come to this church and given the best years
of their lives, in some cases the last productive years and, in one
recent case, the most productive years. Pastors make mistakes.
We are all human. Because we are human, we bleed when cut—
whether it be by rumor, idle gossip, or tone of voice. This church
throughout its history has not always treated its ministers well.
They have been criticized and made fun of when they were sick
and old—openly attacked by callous and condemning tongues.
This is a sin that this congregation has committed, and until we

recognize it as just exactly that and ask God's forgiveness, we are not forgiven.

FOR THE MOST PART, I have not been touched by any of this. I can speak of the men who have served here objectively because I have never met or known any of them.

BUT I DO KNOW YOU! And I do know that we as a congregation are capable of doing great things.

WE ARE A CONGREGATION that ought to weep today. We should weep because we have not done right. We should weep because we have not fulfilled the promises that we made to God. At the baptism of our children, we promised to raise them in the best Christian environment. Our Sunday School is a crowded carnival that would be immediately condemned by any visiting fire marshal.

BY THE GRACE OF GOD, we have been spared seeing our nursery children instantly incinerated in an exploding flash of flame from a baler—because they are trapped in a closed room with a window that cannot open and a coal chute that is wired shut.

IF WE'D HAD a fire in our Sunday School this morning, most of our children would not be sitting in church, would not be alive, because they would have crushed each other to death on the stairs rushing for two tiny exits—because there are so many chairs and tables that there is no room for an aisle.

A primary class would have perished in the cloakroom at the bottom of the stairs, because their door opens outward and would be blocked by pushing children in panic.

THE FIRST-YEAR confirmation class that meets in the kitchen would have rushed out—their door blocking the only exit at the rear of the basement.

AT THE SIGHT OF THEIR SCORCHED skin and shrill screams of terror we would weep. O Lord, we would weep!

WE OUGHT TO WEEP today because we have failed to

grasp the vision that the Kingdom of God finds its strength in its children and we are failing them at Trinity Church.

FAITHFUL TEACHERS spend hours preparing lessons that are never heard because of the crowded confusion. I beg all of you teachers to remain faithful for the love of Jesus—in spite of the conditions under which you must teach children to sing, to pray, and to love God. Be patient, be kind, be a blessing to our children! Please do not leave your job now—whether you are a teacher, an officer, or a leader. Your empty chair will sell innocent souls to a life sick with sin.

WE SHOULD WEEP because the need is here at Trinity. We have made a promise to God to do something about that need. We have pledged ourselves to build a church, but we have not met our budget one month this year. Practicing the most stringent stewardship, counting every postage stamp, every sheet of paper, we have fallen over $225.00 of meeting our bills this month. The little reserve that we have been saving for the future of Trinity is almost gone. Things are so bad that your pastor and treasurer even walked around this building last Thursday evening to see what light bulbs could be removed from the rear of the church in hopes of saving a few pennies.

BUT SAVING PENNIES will not save Trinity Church. The plain facts are this. This congregation will either accept God's grace and God's command and grow or it will die. Our faithful people are getting older. Younger families have no room to come in and shoulder the burden that our Golden Agers have carried far too long.

MANY UGLY things are being said every day. Perhaps you have heard a few of them: "This is my church. We don't need any new people. I never want to see one change made here! If we could get rid of the Children's Home, there would be plenty of room for all of us."

THIS IS SIN. It is sin. It is a sin that is condemning us to death. Trinity Church is going to die. We should weep. For the love of God, we should weep.

THE PARTING WORDS of the president of the Seminary to this pastor, said out of a heart full of love and a life dedicated to the church, were this: "Boys, tell your people to be careful. Many of our congregations are going to hell, because they have pledged their lives to the glory of God and they are cheating God out of their checkbook, out of their children, out of their Christian service."

TODAY by our inaction and sometime giving, we are writing our own epitaph at Trinity Church. Ten or fifteen years from now when our church has crumbled back into the garbage heap —it will be written in the Book of Life—

THERE SAT A PEOPLE OF GOD IN STONY SILENCE.

THEY SATISFIED SATAN.

THEY DID NOT SURVIVE.

LET US PRAY: "O God, may it never be necessary for you to ask me to speak this way to my people again." AMEN.

THE UPPER ROOM

A Silent Room
   A Sharing Room
   A Saving Room

June 7, 1964
   Trinity Lutheran Church, Galion, Ohio
   Trinity II

Holy Communion

TEXT: Mark 14:15

AND HE WILL SHOW you a large upper room furnished and ready; there prepare for us.

"ONCE UPON A TIME" at the beginning of a story usually means that it is not true—or that if it be true, it happened so long ago that it hardly matters anymore.

AND YET, once upon a time, far away and long ago, twelve men and their beloved leader sat around a common table, sharing a common loaf, pouring from a common cup, and hearing from their Lord's lips the most uncommon of words—

This is my body.

This is my blood.

IN THE THEATRE, it is said that dinner scenes are dramatic death. People eating and drinking together just is not interesting. The whole idea of celebrating repeatedly for centuries a solitary supper is, on the surface, preposterous.

LET ME HINT at three things that marked the first Lord's Supper in the upper room. It was A Silent Room, A Sharing Room, and A Saving Room.

IT WAS A SILENT ROOM, on the second story, high above the street. It was a quiet room. Outside, the city was restless. Political agitators were relentlessly darting from one group of men on the sidewalk to another, whispering all of the angry accusations that the crowd would shout in the sunlight of the morning, somewhere in the dull lamplight, a callous and cowardly carpenter drove the final wooden peg into a crude cross. The braying of donkeys, the shriek of a siren, the clatter of hoofs, the monotonous roar of motors—Jerusalem or Galion, does it matter?

OUT OF THE NOISE and confusion of our lives, we need to find a quiet place, a place apart, a place to be alone with God. Great things have come out of the quiet rooms into which men have had the wisdom from time to time to go. Christ chose the upper room. We have chosen to come here this morning. This is our silent room.

THIS IS ALSO A SHARING ROOM. When the disciples walked with Jesus up the twine-thatched ladder to the upper room, they came with the dust of their faults still brown on them. We do not understand the Last Supper if we think that only saints sat around that table. Those men were soul-sick sinners like you and me. Their hands and feet were dirty. Their lives were dirty. Busily eating out of the same pot and sitting on the same stool was Judas with his black intent. Luke says that there was even strife among them that night. The upper room was then and still is a place for men as they are.

WE HAVE COME to this room today to share not only our success, but also our shortcomings and selfish sins. To come here to our Lord's Table demands sincerity—that we be honest with ourselves and recognize just exactly what we are. Jesus demanded that Judas face himself when he handed him the bread and gravy—and Judas had to leave. He could no longer stand to sit with that Christian company once he was found out! When we come to the Table today, we not only face our Lord, but we must face each other, in this—our sharing room.

AS WE COME and listen and share—this becomes a saving room. In the upper room, the disciples came close to Christ. They ate together in the days of food poisoning and foul-poisoning when it was dangerous to eat together. What a remarkable witness to the world—Christians eating and drinking together, Christians in perfect fellowship together!

TODAY IT IS OFTEN IMPOSSIBLE for families to get together at the dinner table because we find that brothers and sisters, mothers and fathers, do not even like each other that much. But we find that at our Lord's Table, sisters will come and stand together, whole families find forgiveness together by the Grace of God. No wonder the world has cherished the Lord's Supper and sought in every century to make it real again. No wonder Maundy Thursday has so much meaning for all of us.

WE HAVE COME HERE TODAY to be close to Christ and each other. That makes this a saving room. Joy, love, peace— these are the gifts Jesus Christ serves to us today in His body and blood. All we have to do is come and we will be forgiven. No matter what we have done, God is telling us today that he is willing to forgive and forget, even though we do not always forget and we do not always forgive.

THIS IS A Silent Room, A Sharing Room, A Saving Room. Come! Join me at the Lord's Table.

AMEN.

UNTITLED SERMON

New Lebanon
  May 15, 1977

HE HIMSELF was the carrier. He had forgotten to examine his own throat.

HOW MUCH EASIER it is to see other people's faults than our own. This blindness to our own imperfections has been the blindness of humanity for centuries.

IN HIS BOOK *Let God In*, Lenn Latham tells a humorous story on himself. He tells of how when he was a child in the second grade at school, the teacher decided to test their sense of touch. She told the class to keep their eyes tightly closed while she passed from desk to desk allowing each student to handle an unidentified object. After each child had a chance to feel it, she would allow them to open their eyes and tell what they thought the object was.

LENN LATHAM told of his impatience as he sat with his eyes tightly closed. Would his turn ever come? In trying to discover what the trouble was, he was horrified to see a boy in the far corner of the room deliberately open his eyes when he thought the teacher's back was turned.

NO SOONER had he seen this than he was on his feet wildly demanding the teacher's attention. "Freddie peeked!" he shouted out. "Freddie peeked!"

I SHALL NEVER FORGET the teacher's thought-provoking reply. She said, "And what were you doing, Lenn?"

NEARLY two thousand years ago, Jesus said to his disciples, "Why do you see the speck that is in your brother's eye, but do not notice the log that is in your own eye?" And then with flawless logic, and even with a touch of humor, he suggested, "First take the log out of your own eye, and then you will see clearly to take the speck out of your brother's eye."

WE ARE TERRIBLY critical of each other, aren't we? As I watch television in the late evenings and talk to my many friends, I often come to the conclusion that we as a society are overly concerned about lint, and dandruff, and bad breath, and underarms! And we purchase endless creams, ointments, roll-ons, and splash-ons—so that we may be strengthened socially, while we totally forget that if we are to be assured of our salvation we must become strengthened in the Spirit.

SOCIALLY WE MAY SMELL SWEET and be cleaner than white rain—and at the same time spiritually be a stench that shakes the very gates of Heaven. I am constantly amazed at our human ability to feel that we are right all of the time—and that everyone else is totally wrong most of the time.

SAINT PAUL is praying the prayer of our text for each of us this morning. Of all the apostles, Paul could most speak of the Glory of the Christ-life, for he had seen all of it concentrated into one bright light on the Damascus road. It was splendid! It was glorious! It blinded him! Paul prays fervently that every one of us might become so strengthened in spirit that we might become blinded by the love and power of Christ.

WHEN WE LOOK into the hallway mirror, far too often we are blinded more by the magnificence of ourselves than by the light of Christ shining out of our lives.

IF WE ARE TO BECOME strengthened in spirit, first we will have to take a good look at ourselves—at our earthly lives—at our spiritual lives. When we think others are looking, we tend to "spruce up a bit" and make all of those minor repairs that we think are necessary for happy living. Saturday, a week ago, while a friend and I were in Columbus, we happened to observe a delightful lady making repairs at the lunch counter of the five and dime. After finishing her soup and coffee, she produced with the agility of a sleight-of-hand artist—a mirror, a lipstick, a comb, and a can of white powder, and a yellow Kleenex. Now I am sure that this same lady would be indignant if she found a fingernail in her soup—but she did not bat an eyelash as she spilled powder all over the pie on the counter and combed loose hair onto the floor. She was so busy looking at herself that she was totally blinded to the spectacle that she was creating for all to see.

ONE YOUNG MAN was trying to break away from a life of open immorality. But in spite of all his firm resolves, he invariably suffered relapses. "I'll admit, I drink," he said to his minister, "and I run around with women. But at least," he hastened to say, "I'm honest about it. I'm not like most church people; I'm no hypocrite!"

DO YOU SEE what happens to us when we compare ourselves with other human beings? After a while, we all tend to look alike—and to think alike. St. Paul prays that we compare ourselves only to Christ and become rooted and grounded in the Spirit of God. It is not Paul's prayer that we become arrayed in the love of this Spring's bright yellow fashions or be padded by Brooks Brothers. It is Paul's prayer that we become arrayed in the love of Christ and that we may be filled with the fullness of God.

GOD'S LOVE—that ought to be our height, and depth, and length, and breadth. Nothing else will make us strong in the spirit.

MUCH OF OUR TROUBLE arises out of our inclination to compare and contrast ourselves with other human beings—who are imperfect. What snobs we become when we measure each other according to ourselves. It is only in a society like ours that children can think their fathers or mothers are stupid or ignorant, or out of touch with the times—just because the children seem to learn more in school.

WE NEED an absolutely perfect standard by which to measure ourselves. Imagine the chaos that would arise in commerce, or in the building industry, or in our daily lives if every individual were free to determine the length of his own foot ruler.

FOR EXAMPLE, any man measuring his height with a short ruler—say ten inches—might easily be deluded into thinking that he is taller than he really is.

TO AVOID CONFUSION, the Bureau of Standards in Washington, D.C. maintains a measuring unit that is one absolute standard for all the foot rulers in the United States. If any citizen is in doubt as to whether a particular measure is exactly one-foot-long, all he needs to do is have it compared with the one perfect standard in Washington.

GOD HAS WISELY provided us with the one perfect standard by which we can measure our lives. That perfect standard is Jesus Christ. We can gain an accurate picture of our personality only as we measure ourselves by him.

He is the one power that can strengthen our spiritual lives. He is willing to do for each one of us far more abundantly than we can ask or think. This is Paul's prayer for us—that we be strengthened in the Spirit of Christ.

IT IS PAUL'S PRAYER. It is and will be our life—when we look away from ourselves and our neighbor—and all of our petty faults and failures—and look to Christ alone.

AMEN.

POETRY

THE THINKING COUCH

Serpentine I lie on my thinking couch.
  Satisfied.
  Safe.
  Coiled and choosing not to think.
  Clearly Master of my thinking couch.

"There is no God!" shouts a Crazy Man chasing ghosts with a swatter.
  "There is no God!" Swat! Swat!
  "There is no God!" Swat! Swat! *Swat!*

"If there is *no* God," serenely I say, "there would be *no* ghosts for you to chase."
  The swatting stops.
  The swatter drops.

The Crazy Man stumbles from my thinking space.

Silent I and my new swatter lie.

Satisfied.

Safe.

Swatting ghosts would be *my* mission.

"This is a perfect thinking couch," I think.

Coiled and choosing not to think.

LETTERS

ON THE DEATH OF HIS MOTHER

February 10, 1988

Dearest Helen,

It has been one week today since Grandma Betcher died. We miss her very much.

I arrived in Dallas quite late, as the airplane had difficulty in St. Louis and had to be repaired. There was no time to change clothes, so I am fortunate that I put on my black suit for the trip. Paul and Terry picked me up at the airport and took me to Restland and left me at the room where Mother was.

I had about a half hour alone with Mother before they moved the casket to the chapel for the funeral.

Mother and I had a long talk. I am so fortunate that I had this little bit of time to spend with her alone before she was buried. I pulled a chair up to the casket and chatted with her like I had done so often before when she was alive.

The room at Restland was lovely. Grandma would have loved it. On each side of Grandma were twin baskets of flowers from her beloved grandchildren. They were very large white mums with nice greenery—a pink bow from the girls and a blue bow from the boys.

Grandma looked beautiful. There were no wrinkles on her face or pain lines. My sister did her makeup, and she had a bouquet of red roses in her hand. We are so fortunate that in her last hours she had no pain or suffering. I told Grandma during our talk how much you wanted to be there and how hard you have been working at school. She liked that.

There were flowers everywhere. There was a large white standing spray of flowers from your father's Columbus friends. It had a gold bow. There were many baskets and about seven flowering plants that are now here at the house.

My sister and I placed a spray of one hundred red roses on top of the casket when it was moved to the chapel for the funeral service. They were quite beautiful, and of course, Mother's favorite. There were several different kinds of red roses in the spray, which gave it variety and even more beauty.

Pastor Nichols of Concordia Lutheran Church presided at the funeral service. He likened Grandma to a rose who accepted the beauty of life with all of its flowers *and* thorns.

Grandma was buried during a snowstorm in a grave facing a large white statue of Jesus. How fitting that it snowed! It reminded me or our Pennsylvania winters. I am sure Grandma was pleased.

The neighbors brought in so much food that most of it is still in the freezer. Dad and I have gained about ten pounds. I have never seen such an outpouring of love. It has been a tribute to Grandma.

On Sunday morning, Dad and I attended Concordia Lutheran Church, where Grandma was remembered again. Pastor Nichols preached on the theme *I Never Promised You a Rose Garden*.

Grandma is gone, and we miss her. Pepper is still looking all over the house for her. Grandpa is often forgetful but is doing better than I expected he would.

I love you so much and am anxious to come home tomorrow. Grandma is at peace and so am I.

Love,
   Daddy

ON HIS FATHER'S DEATH

February 24, 1995

Dear Eric,

It was the day of your great grandma's funeral that I first took notice of the condition of your great grandpa, who was my dad.

At the house after the funeral, Dad drank too much. He told a neighbor girl that she could no longer visit him, because he did not want to become known as a molester of children. She looked stunned. I was standing beside him as he introduced Jim Beene, a neighbor and good friend, as his son—the son he always wanted.

After your great grandma died, I learned many things about Dad that Mother had kept well hidden. I did not know that Dad was an alcoholic.

My Grandma Ada told me that my Grandpa Betcher, who I do not remember, was an alcoholic. My grandpa shot himself while drunk, after shooting his pistol out the second story window of the family home at nothing in particular. Grandma Ada cried after she told me about my grandpa because she'd been told never to tell me about his death. I thanked her for filling in another blank in my life and never betrayed her indiscretion.

Neither Mother nor Dad ever told me about Grandpa Betcher. Nothing was said even when Mary Jane—Dad's brother's daughter—hanged herself in the basement. They told me that Mary Jane had an accident while "practicing to hang herself."

That made as much sense as most things did in the confusion of those absurd and annoying adolescent years. I remained an adolescent until I was about thirty-five years old.

I was in college when Mary Jane practiced hanging herself. I was still rather naïve and had just found "religion." My Aunt Bea, who also had "religion," wept when I placed a small leather testament with gold glitter edges in Mary Jane's casket. She said it was the "nicest damned thing" she'd ever seen. I took it as a compliment. After all, we had "religion!"

My dad's brother David was also an alcoholic. Uncle David was an interesting man. He was movie star handsome, tanned, dapper dressed, and a talented musician. He played the organ on the radio when everything was broadcast live. He played dinner music every night for thirty minutes. In the evenings, he played in night clubs and drank until dawn. The after hours people tipped well, which kept Uncle David tippling well.

Uncle David's wife, Bea, had a sister with purple lips. She lived with them in Mt. Lebanon, which was a ritzy section of Pittsburgh at that time. I thought it was a hoot. Uncle David had a red nose, and Aunt Bea, who prided herself on being piss elegant, had a sister with purple lips!

I was too young to make the connection that those think purple lips indicated a serious heart condition, Nor did I make the connection that the scales on the back of Uncle David's hands were a sign of his alcohol disease. Those observations came much later after many pastoral counseling sessions.

Listening for endless hours to humankind recite the misery of body and mind was an excellent education. I was no longer an adolescent but not yet a man.

I found out about my dad's drinking problem when my sister told me he had fallen off the toilet and broken several ribs. It was evident he could no longer care for himself.

Dad moved to a lovely apartment at Presbyterian Village, which he hated. He received one hot meal a day in the dining room, which had cloth table coverings and napkins. At his first dinner, Dad stirred his coffee with his iced tea spoon and left the spoon in the cup. There was a bowl of creamers on the table. Dad needed only one for his coffee, yet he opened each one in the bowl and drank it. He sipped and savored each, smacking his lips in wild abandon.

Shortly after Dad moved into Presbyterian Village, I received the only piece of mail I ever got from him after Mother died. There was no personal note. It was a copy of the resident newsletter containing an article about him, including a long section about his daughter who was a registered nurse and her sons, Terry and Brian. There was no mention that he had a son in Ohio and two beautiful granddaughters in Colorado.

I have no clue why he sent the newsletter to me. I have wondered wistfully if he was sending me a message of some sort.

Dad was known as the "whistler" by the other residents. He whistled and tap danced up and down the uncarpeted halls. He bathed at night to keep his sheets clean, even though my sister washed them weekly.

Daily, Dad jumped from bed at 5:30 a.m., got dressed, and sat in his chair because he was afraid he'd be late for lunch, which was served at noon. Dad was always first in the lunch line. He was very proud of that! When I visited, he got in line and went into the dining room to begin eating, leaving me in the assembly area waiting for my sister to complete her volunteer duties and join us for lunch.

Dad would take no medication until the duty nurse called his RN daughter and received her permission for the proffered medication.

When he was younger, Dad sang in a church music group and starred in amateur musicals. At Presbyterian, Dad took an interest in the men's chorus. He told the volunteer choir director that he was a professional singer and insisted the choir sing in harmony and not in unison. The director, who delighted in getting the chorus to sing the same note or word at the same time, told Dad his skills were beyond those of the chorus and asked him not to return. Dad accepted that as a compliment.

Dad walked and whistled one mile every day in the halls of his building. He continued until his health began to deteriorate.

In January 1992, Dad moved to the health care section. He had a private room, carpeted floors, two new reclining chairs, his pictures, ad his own television. He loathed it. He felt as if he were in jail.

His health continued to decline. Dad wanted to die, and death delayed.

I visited Dallas when Dad went into the hospital for minor surgery. His health failed quickly. We talked more the last day I saw him than we ever had. We made peace, and I was pleased.

I told him it was okay to die and to go be with Mom if that was what he wanted. Tears washed my face when he started holding his breath. Dad tried so hard to die that day. He held his breath, and all I could do was hold his hand.

A hospital caregiver came by and asked if I wanted to see the chaplain. "I am the chaplain," I said. Silently, she slipped away from my sorrow.

My sister planned the funeral. When Mother died, she arranged to have her in a chapel room, held family visiting hours, and placed a spray of one hundred red roses on her casket. Dad had no calling hours and lay in a cubicle with a lamp. He got a spray of something not remembered from "all of us."

Dad's funeral was both beautiful and bizarre.

Dad had already been moved to Wildwood Chapel for the funeral, and the casket was closed before I arrived. Pastor Nichols quietly talked about Dad. It was evident that he knew my father better than any of us.

I was ashamed.

Only the immediate family went to the gravesite. My nephews were hungry. We left before the casket was lowered into the ground.

I was ashamed.

My dad, your great grandpa, lies peacefully with your great grandma at Restland Memorial Gardens.

Love,

Grandpa Bill

ON HIS GRANDSON'S FIRST CHRISTMAS

December 25, 1993

Dear Eric,

It's Christmas, Eric!

It's your *first* Christmas! You have been born into a whistling world of color and clatter. Already you are reaching out for shapes, shadows, and things that go bump. You find it all so interesting. You are not afraid.

You smile, giggle, and laugh.

Your mission, Eric, is to help others smile with you. You have been chosen to bring Christmas to the lost and lonely.

You have brought a special sparkle to the eyes of your dear mother and father. You are happy. Your immediate mission is to keep them smiling during difficult days.

You are fortune. You were born smiling. Everyone who meets you smiles, giggles, and laughs. Even your grandpa finds reason to smile.

You are special I have looked into your eyes. I *like* what I see shining back. Mother God has given you gifts and a mission.

I must tell you, Eric, that you have more gifts than you now recognize. It will take your entire life to find all of the gifts under your tree today. The colors, carols, and charisma of Christmas will be twinkling out of your eyes every day of the year.

Those who have the fortune to meet you as you walk through life's avenues and alleys will be different for having the experience. Countless creatures will meet you, Eric, because you will be seeking out the lost dogs of the world. You will be found in interesting, and sometimes dangerous, places.

You will always be where people gather. You will look into their eyes and recognize pain. You will smile and listen. It may only be a chance passing—a time frozen fragment—but they will walk away smiling *your* smile and feeling less pain.

Along with the gift of smiling you have been born to be a talker. Talking runs in the family. You will talk to those you meet on the street, at the mall, in life's lines, on elevators, and everywhere.

Life for you promises a thrilling dialogue with dogs, the invisible poor, the wealthy, and others who have forgotten to smile and fear shapes, shadows, and things that go bump.

Christmas is about *gifts*, Eric!

You have been chosen to take Christmas everywhere you go.

When you meet Mother God's children, you will *make* them look into your eyes and smile. Often you will not say a word. However, when that child walks away from an encounter with you, she or he will *never* be the same.

It's your first Christmas, Eric, and *you* are the gift under the world's tree!

Love always,
    Grandpa Bill

Editor's Note:
    My son Eric is now twenty-seven years old. My father's assessment of him and what he'd bring to the world turned out

to be eerily accurate. As a baby, he made even the crankiest old men smile. As a child, he talked to everyone he met and was always the center of attention. As he grew and his musical gifts surfaced, he became a performer who never knew stage fright. His charisma fills a room, and audiences smile and laugh when he performs on stage.

Find him at www.ericjmcconnell.com.

ACKNOWLEDGMENTS

Thank you first to my late father for the material that graces these pages. I wish he had produced more that I could share, and I wish he'd lived his dream of writing and publishing during his lifetime. Had he believed in himself and used his talent, he could have moved mountains.

Thank you to my mother, Elise Freitag Tom, for all the memories of my father shared with me over the years.

Thank you to my son Eric McConnell, who typed my father's work onto the computer for me.

Thank you to my cover artist, Marci Clark, for bringing my vision to life beautifully and expediently.

And thank *you*, whoever is reading this. I hope my father's words speak to you.

Helen Hardt

ABOUT THE AUTHOR

William Charles Betcher (1936-2015) grew up in the Pennsylvania hills with his parents and younger sister. He excelled academically and was a gifted writer and artist. He attended Capital University and Trinity Lutheran Seminary in Columbus, Ohio. In 1962, he married Elise Freitag of Baltimore. He served as minister for several parishes in Ohio before resigning from the ministry in the late seventies. He continued his career at the Ohio Civil Rights Commission, where he served as Southeast Regional Director and subsequently Chief of Compliance until he retired on disability in the early 2000s. He was the father of #1 *New York Times* bestselling author Helen Hardt and Colorado attorney Louise Betcher Staab, and grandfather to four. Though he was a gifted writer, Betcher never published during his lifetime.

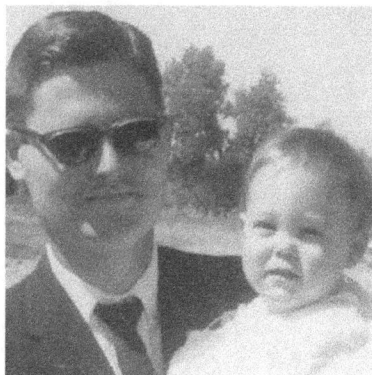

ABOUT THE EDITOR

#1 *New York Times*, #1 *USA Today*, and #1 *Wall Street Journal* best-selling author Helen Hardt's passion for the written word began with the books her mother read to her at bedtime. She wrote her first story at age six and hasn't stopped since. In addition to being an award-winning author of romantic fiction, she's a mother, an attorney, a black belt in Taekwondo, a grammar geek, an appreciator of fine red wine, and a lover of Ben and Jerry's ice cream. She writes from her home in Colorado, where she lives with her family. Her father, William Charles Betcher, was her first mentor.

PRAISE FOR HELEN HARDT

STEEL BROTHERS SAGA

"Craving is the jaw-dropping book you *need* to read!"
~*New York Times* bestselling author Lisa Renee Jones

"Completely raw and addictive."
~#1 *New York Times* bestselling author Meredith Wild

"Talon has hit my top five list...up there next to Jamie Fraser and Gideon Cross."
~*USA Today* bestselling author Angel Payne

"Talon and Jade's instant chemistry heats up the pages..."
~RT Book Reviews

"Sorry Christian and Gideon, there's a new heartthrob for you to contend with. Meet Talon. Talon Steel."
~Booktopia

"Such a beautiful torment—the waiting, the anticipation, the relief that only comes briefly before more questions arise, and the wait begins again... Check. Mate. Ms. Hardt..."
~**Bare Naked Words**

"Made my heart stop in my chest. Helen has given us such a heartbreakingly beautiful series."
~**Tina, Bookalicious Babes**

WOLFES OF MANHATTAN

"It's hot, it's intense, and the plot starts off thick and had me completely spellbound from page one."
~**The Sassy Nerd Blog**

"Helen Hardt...is a master at her craft."
~**K. Ogburn, Amazon**

"Move over Steel brothers... Rock is *everything!*"
~**Barbara Conklin-Jaros, Amazon**

"Helen has done it again. She winds you up and weaves a web of intrigue."
~**Vicki Smith, Amazon**

FOLLOW ME SERIES

"Hardt spins erotic gold..."
~*Publishers Weekly*

"22 Best Erotic Novels to Read"
~*Marie Claire* **Magazine**

"Intensely erotic and wildly emotional..."
~*New York Times* **bestselling author Lisa Renee Jones**

"With an edgy, enigmatic hero and loads of sexual tension, Helen Hardt's fast-paced Follow Me Darkly had me turning pages late into the night!"
~*New York Times* **bestselling author J. Kenner**

"Christian, Gideon, and now...Braden Black."
~**Books, Wine, and Besties**

"A tour de force where the reader will be pulled in as if they're being seduced by Braden Black, taken for a wild ride, and left wanting more."
~*USA Today* **Bestselling Author Julie Morgan**

"Hot. Sexy. Intriguing. Page-Turner. Helen Hardt checks all the boxes with *Follow Me Darkly!*"
~**International Bestselling Author Victoria Blue**

BLOOD BOND SAGA

"An enthralling and rousing vampire tale that will leave readers waiting for the sequel."
~**Kirkus Reviews**

"Dangerous and sexy. A new favorite!"
~*New York Times* **bestselling author Alyssa Day**

"Helen gives us the dark, tormented vampire hero we all love in a sensual paranormal romance with all the feels. Be warned... The twists and turns will keep you up all night reading. I was hooked from the first sentence until the very end."

~*New York Times* bestselling author J.S. Scott

"A dark, intoxicating tale."
~**Library Journal**

"Helen dives into the paranormal world of vampires and makes it her own."
~**Tina, Bookalicious Babes**

"Throw out everything you know about vampires—except for that blood thirst we all love and lust after in these stunning heroes—and expect to be swept up in a sensual story that twists and turns in so many wonderfully jaw-dropping ways."
~**Angel Payne,** *USA Today* **bestselling author**

BY HELEN HARDT

Steel Brothers Saga:
Trilogy One—Talon and Jade
Craving
Obsession
Possession
Trilogy Two—Jonah and Melanie
Melt
Burn
Surrender
Trilogy Three—Ryan and Ruby
Shattered
Twisted
Unraveled
Trilogy Four—Bryce and Marjorie
Breathless
Ravenous
Insatiable
Trilogy Five—Brad and Daphne
Fate
Legacy

Descent
Trilogy Six—Dale and Ashley (coming soon)
Awakened
Cherished
Freed

Follow Me Series:
Follow Me Darkly
Follow Me Under (coming soon)
Follow Me Always (coming soon)

Wolfes of Manhattan:
Rebel
Recluse
Runaway
Rake (coming soon)
Reckoning (coming soon)

Blood Bond Saga:
Unchained
Unhinged
Undaunted
Unmasked
Undefeated

Sex and the Season:
Lily and the Duke
Rose in Bloom
Lady Alexandra's Lover
Sophie's Voice

Temptation Saga:
Tempting Dusty

Teasing Annie
Taking Catie
Taming Angelina
Treasuring Amber
Trusting Sydney
Tantalizing Maria

Standalone Novels and Novellas
Reunited

Misadventures:
Misadventures of a Good Wife (with Meredith Wild)
Misadventures with a Rockstar

The Cougar Chronicles:
The Cowboy and the Cougar
Calendar Boy

Daughters of the Prairie:
The Outlaw's Angel
Lessons of the Heart
Song of the Raven

Collections:
Destination Desire
Her Two Lovers

Non-Fiction:
got style?

www.ingramcontent.com/pod-product-compliance
Lightning Source LLC
LaVergne TN
LVHW041314080426
835513LV00008B/460